ADVANCED lighthouse 1

Grammarmaster

Deinen Grammarmaster findest du auch in der **Cornelsen Lernen App**.

Siehst du eines dieser Symbole in deinem Grammarmaster, findest du in der App …

- alle **Audios**
- alle **Erklärfilme**
- **Lösungen** zu den Aufgaben

Cornelsen

ADVANCED
lighthouse 1

Grammarmaster

Im Auftrag des Verlages erarbeitet von
Gwen Berwick, York
Sydney Thorne, York

In Zusammenarbeit mit der Englischredaktion
Klaus Unger (Projektleitung), Anja Zieschang

Beratende Mitwirkung
Daniel Henn, Frankfurt/Main; Christina Sieber, Schorndorf

Lizenzmanagement
Silke Kirchhoff

Illustrationen
Evelt Yanait, Advocate Art

Fotos
Anja Poehlmann, Brighton
Für die freundliche Unterstützung danken wir der Varndean School, Brighton

Umschlaggestaltung
Rosendahl, Berlin

Layoutkonzept
Klein & Halm, Berlin

Layout und technische Umsetzung
Straive

Druck
AZ Druck und Datentechnik GmbH, Kempten

PEFC
PEFC/04-31-2260
PEFC-zertifiziert
Dieses Produkt stammt aus nachhaltig bewirtschafteten Wäldern und kontrollierten Quellen
www.pefc.de

www.cornelsen.de

1. Auflage, 1. Druck 2023
978-3-06-034606-6

So lernst du mit Lighthouse U2
Impressum 2
Inhaltsverzeichnis 3

Unit 1
My new school
Der unbestimmte Artikel: *a/an* 4
A/an vor Vokalen 5
Der bestimmte Artikel: *the* 5
Der Plural der Nomen 6
Der Plural der Nomen: Formen 7
Die Personalpronomen 8
Das Verb *be*: Bejahte Aussagesätze 10
Das Verb *be*: Verneinte Aussagesätze 12
Der s-Genitiv 14
Die *of*-Fügung 15

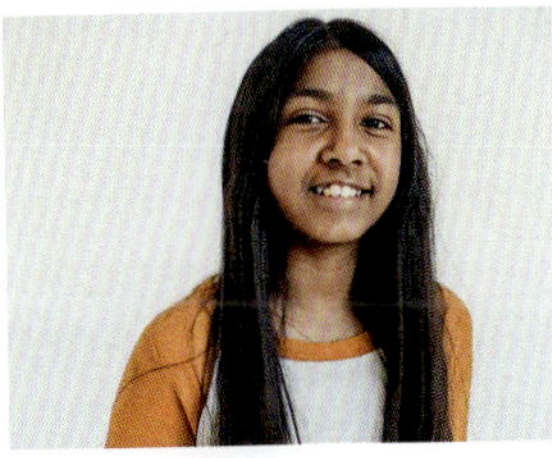

Unit 2
My family and home
Das Verb *be*: Fragen und Kurzantworten 17
There is ... / There are ... 20
Possessivbegleiter 21

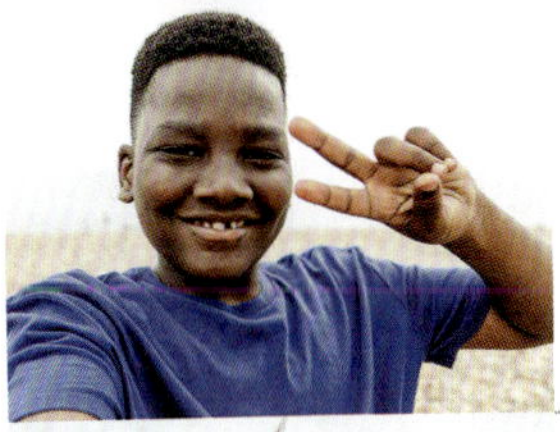

Unit 3
My day
Das simple present: Bejahte Aussagesätze 23
Das simple present: Sonderformen 26
Die Wortstellung 27

Unit 4
Where I live
Das simple present: Verneinte Aussagesätze 46
Das simple present: Fragen und Kurzantworten 50
Das simple present: Fragen mit Fragewörtern 52

Unit 5
Enjoy!
Das present progressive: Bejahte Aussagesätze 55
Die *ing*-Form: Schreibung 56
Das present progressive: Verneinte Aussagesätze und Fragen 57
much – many – a lot of 59

Auf einen Blick 64

Lösungen 29
Quellenverzeichnis 72

Unit 1
My new school

Der unbestimmte Artikel: *a/an*

Der unbestimmte Artikel (ein, eine) heißt im Englischen a oder an.
Du verwendest
- a, wenn das folgende Wort mit einem Konsonanten (b, c, d, ..., z) beginnt,
  a boy – ein Junge a car – ein Auto
- an, wenn das folgende Wort mit einem Vokal (a, e, i, o, u) beginnt.
  an animal – ein Tier an exercise book – ein Heft

! Substantive (*boy, car, rabbit*) schreibst du (anders als im Deutschen) klein.

► SB p. 21, p. 203

1 T-shirts

a) **What picture is on the T-shirt? Write the words with *a* or *an* under the right picture.**
Was siehst du auf dem T-Shirt? Schreibe die Wörter mit a *oder* an *unter die Bilder.*

1 
a lion

2 
______

3 
______

4 
______

5 
______

6 
______

7 
______

8 
______

b) **Complete the sentences. Write *a* or *an*.** *Vervollständige die Sätze. Schreibe* a *oder* an.

1 ____ horse is ____ animal. ____ elephant is ____ animal too.

2 You can eat ____ apple. But you can't eat ____ glue stick! Yuk!

3 I can see ____ zebra, ____ gorilla and ____ orang utan.

Zebra, gorilla und *orang utan* sind neue Wörter, aber keine Angst! Dank deiner Grammatikkenntnisse weißt du, welcher der richtige Artikel (*a* oder *an*) ist.

► Check

A/an vor Vokalen

Vorsicht bei vorgeschobenen Adjektiven, die mit einem Vokal (a, e, i, o, u) beginnen.
I have a dog. It's an old dog. – Ich habe einen Hund. Er ist ein alter Hund.

Bei der Wahl von a oder an ist die Aussprache entscheidend, nicht die Schreibweise, also:

a uniform [ˈjuːnɪfɔːm] – eine Uniform	... weil das gesprochene Wort mit einem
a unit [ˈjuːnɪt] – eine Lerneinheit	Konsonanten [j] beginnt
Aber: *an hour [ˈaʊə(r)] – eine Stunde*	... weil das gesprochene Wort mit [aʊ] beginnt

► SB p. 21, p. 203

2 At school

Circle the right word: *a* or *an*. *Kreise das richtige Wort ein:* a *oder* an.

1 I have a / an book. It's a / an big book. It's a / an English book.

2 And I have a / an pencil. It's a / an old pencil, but I like it.

3 I have a / an exercise book. It's a / an orange exercise book.

4 We have a / an uniform. It's a / an blue and grey uniform.

5 'My new school' is a / an unit in my English book. It's a / an good unit.

Der bestimmte Artikel: *the*

Du sprichst den bestimmten Artikel the (der, die, das):
- [ðə], vor einem Wort, das mit einem Konsonanten beginnt: *the [ðə] teacher, the [ðə] car*
- [ði], vor einem Wort, das mit einem Vokal beginnt: *the [ði] animal, the [ði] apple*

► SB p. 21, p. 203

3 Mr Lee's sentences

a) **First, highlight the letters in bold: blue for a consonant, red for a vowel.** *Markiere die fett gedruckten Buchstaben: blau für einen Konsonanten, rot für einen Vokal.*

b) **Then tick the right column: [ðə] or [ði].** *Hake die richtige Spalte ab: [ðə] oder [ði].*

	ðə	ði	ðə	ði
1 Look at the **b**oard!	✓	☐		
2 Open the **b**ook at page 21.	☐	☐		
3 Eat the **a**pple, please.	☐	☐		
4 Listen to the **m**usic and to the **E**nglish students.	☐	☐	☐	☐
5 Look at the **p**icture of the **o**ld horse.	☐	☐	☐	☐

c) **Now read the sentences aloud. Take care with 'the'.** *Lies die Sätze laut vor. Achte auf „the".*

► Check

Der Plural der Nomen

An die meisten Nomen wird im Plural -s angehängt.

a dog → two dogs – ein Hund, zwei Hunde

a cat → three cats – eine Katze, drei Katzen

! Sonderformen:

one child → two children – Kind / Kinder
one man → two men – Mann / Männer
one woman → two women – Frau / Frauen

I have a mouse. → I like mice. – Maus / Mäuse
I have a fish. → I like fish. – Fisch / Fische
I have a sheep. → I like sheep. – Schaf / Schafe

Ein paar wenige Nomen haben keine Singularform und werden nur im Plural gebraucht:
people – Menschen *trousers – Hose* *clothes – Kleidung*

► SB p. 22, p. 203

4 Sunita is at the zoo

Write the correct words in the plural. There are two extra words in the box.
Schreibe die Wörter im Plural. Zwei Wörter aus dem Kasten brauchst du nicht.

child • ~~elephant~~ • fish • horse • lion • man • parrot • snake • woman

I can see two *elephants*, three ____________, four ____________,

five ____________, six ____________, seven ____________

and eight ____________.

► Check

Der Plural der Nomen: Formen

Die Folgenden sind die drei wichtigsten Pluralformen:

1 die meisten Nomen + -s	2 -s, -x, -ch oder -sh + -es	3 Vokal + y + -s
a lion → two lions	*a bus → two buses*	*a boy → two boys*
a year → three years	*a beach → two beaches*	
		Konsonant + y wird zu -ies
		a story → two stories
		a pony → two ponies

▸ SB p. 22, p. 203

5 Words with -y

a) **Look at the words in b. Highlight the letters in bold: blue for a consonant, red for a vowel.**
Schau dir die Wörter bei b an. Markiere die fett gedruckten Buchstaben: blau für einen Konsonanten, rot für einen Vokal.

b) **Write the correct plural forms in Amira's poster: *-s* or *-ies*.** *Schreibe die richtigen Pluralformen in Amiras Poster: -s oder -ies.*

holid**ay**
hob**by**
monk**ey**
po**ny**

I like (1) ______________________.

I have two (2) ______________________:

swimming and coding.

I don't like (3) ______________________.

My favourite animals are (4) ______________________.

6 More than one

a) **Look again at the grammar box. Then read the highlighted words in b. Are they in group 1, 2, or 3?**
Schau dir den Grammatikkasten noch einmal an. Lies dann die markierten Wörter in b. Gehören sie zu Gruppe 1, 2 oder 3?

b) **Complete the sentences with the plural of the words.**
Vervollständige die Sätze mit dem Plural der Wörter.

1 friend 1 Hassan and Sasha are my ______________.

2 baby ____ I love ______________.

3 box ____ Look at the words in the two ______________.

4 sandwich ____ I eat ______________ at school.

5 pen, pencil ____ I have two __________ and three __________ in my pencil case.

6 party ____ ______________ are great!

▸ Check

Die Personalpronomen

Personalpronomen ersetzen Nomen oder Eigennamen. Die Personalpronomen sind:

I (ich)	we (wir)
you (du, Sie)	you (ihr, Sie)
he (er)	they (sie)
she (sie)	
it (es)	

! Das Pronomen I (ich) wird im Englischen immer großgeschrieben.
Das Pronomen it steht für Dinge und Tiere und entspricht „er“, „sie“ oder „es“:
I have a guitar. ~~The guitar~~ It's great.
What page is it?

► SB p. 24, p. 204

7 My new school

Replace the phrases with the right pronouns.
Ersetze die Satzglieder durch die richtigen Personalpronomen.

1 I have a new timetable. ~~The timetable~~ ______________ is OK.

2 My class teacher is Ms Ahmed. ~~Ms Ahmed~~ ______________ is nice.

3 My friends and I are in the same class. ~~My friends and I~~ ______________ are in 7B.

4 Max is a student in my class. ~~Max~~ ______________ is from Oxford.

5 Look! Livvy and Dan are very tired. ~~Livvy and Dan~~ ______________ are asleep.

8 At school

Match sentences 1–7 with the right sentences A–G. Write the sentences.
Ordne die Sätze 1–7 den Sätzen A–G zu. Schreibe die Sätze.

~~A She's great.~~
B Here it is.
C They're in room 11.
D We're four good friends.
E He's in the classroom.
F Yes, I have my uniform and my school bag.
G It's blue and grey.

Achte in den Sätzen A–G auf die Personalpronomen. Das hilft dir, die richtige Zuordnung zu finden.

1 I like Sunita. – *She's great.*

2 We have a school uniform. – ______________________________

3 Can I have your pen, please? – ______________________________

4 Where's Zane? – ______________________________

5 Where are the English lessons? – ______________________________

6 Are you ready for school, Noah? – ______________________________

7 I like Lily, Emma and Tim. – ______________________________

► Check

☒ 9 Sunita, Lily, Noah and Zane at school

Complete the photo story with the correct pronouns. *Vervollständige die Fotogeschichte mit den richtigen Personalpronomen.*

It's lunch break at Varndean …

► Check

Erklär-film

Das Verb *be*: Bejahte Aussagesätze

Es gibt zwei Formen von be: Kurzformen *(short forms)* und Langformen *(long forms)*. Bei den Kurzformen ersetzt ein Apostroph (’) einen weggefallenen Buchstaben.

	Langformen	Kurzformen	
• bei offiziellen Schreiben • nach Eigennamen *(Zane, Sunita)* • nach Nomen *(bike, teachers)*	I am you are he is / she is / it is we are you are they are	I’m you’re he’s / she’s / it’s we’re you’re they’re	• beim Sprechen • in persönlichen E-Mails oder Chats • nach Pronomen: *(I, you, he, she, it, we, you, they)*

► SB p. 24, p. 205

10 Where are you from?

Circle the correct short form of *be*. *Kreise die richtige Kurzform von be ein.*

1 Where are you from, Milo and Oliver?

– We ’m / ’s / ’re from Brighton.

2 And you ’m / ’s / ’re from Brighton too, right, Ivy?

– No, I ’m / ’s / ’re from Leeds.

3 And where is Zahra from?

– She ’m / ’s / ’re from London.

4 Where are Lin and Kiera from?

– They ’m / ’s / ’re from Oxford.

5 Where is Jason from?

– He ’m / ’s / ’re from Manchester.

11 Class 7C

Write the correct form of *be*: *is* or *are*. *Schreibe die richtige Form von* be: is *oder* are.

1 Sarah and I __________ in 7C.

2 But all my other friends __________ all in 7K.

3 My maths teacher __________ Ms Khan.

4 Art and PE __________ two subjects at my school.

5 Assembly __________ on Tuesday and Thursday.

6 The timetable __________ OK.

Überlege, durch welches Personalpronomen du das Satzglied vor der Lücke ersetzen kannst. Das hilft dir, die richtige Form von *be* zu finden.

► Check

12 Class 7K

Write the sentences in blue in the short form of *be*.
Schreibe die Sätze in Blau in der Kurzform von be.

Mia Is your class OK, Jack?

Jack 1 Yes, I like the students in my class.

They are nice. *They're nice.*

2 We are 25 students in 7K.

____

3 I have a good friend, Olga. She is nice. _______________

4 My friend Zack is nice too. He is from London. _______________

5 I am happy in my class. _______________

Mia Thank you, Jack!

Jack You are welcome, Mia! _______________

13 Two messages

a) **Complete the messages with *'m, 's* or *'re*.** *Vervollständige die Nachrichten mit* 'm, 's *oder* 're.

Hi, Nazim. I ________ (1) in London with Dad. It ________ (2) nice here. We ________ (3) in London Zoo. I like the monkeys. They ________ (4) great! ☺
See you soon. Kinga

Hi, Kinga. You ________ (5) lucky. I ________ (6) in Brighton and I can't go swimming with Mum. She ________ (7) tired. And I can't play basketball with Lily and Zane. They ________ (8) busy.

b) **Now write the long forms of *be*.** *Schreibe die Langformen von* be.

1 Kinga ________ lucky.

2 She and her dad ________ in London Zoo.

3 It ________ nice there.

4 The monkeys ________ great.

5 But Nazim ________ in Brighton and his mum ________ tired.

6 And Lily and Zane ________ busy.

▸ Check

Erklär-film

Das Verb *be*: Verneinte Aussagesätze

Es gibt wieder zwei Formen, wobei fast immer die Kurzformen benutzt werden.

Langformen	Kurzformen
I am not very big.	I'm not very big.
You are not very big.	You aren't very big.
He is not very big.	He isn't very big.
She is not very big.	She isn't very big.
It is not very big.	It isn't very big.
We are not very big.	We aren't very big.
You are not very big.	You aren't very big.
They are not very big.	They aren't very big.

▶ SB p. 29, p. 205

14 Nice or not nice?

Circle the correct negative form of the verb *be*. *Kreise die richtige Verneinung des Verbs* be *ein.*

1

We 'm not / isn't / aren't busy.

2

Parkour 'm not / isn't / aren't hard.

3

I 'm not / isn't / aren't lucky!

4

The cats 'm not / isn't / aren't very happy!

5

Nav 'm not / isn't / aren't good at yoga.

6

It 'm not / isn't / aren't great here!

▶ Check

15 At school

Match the sentence parts and write the right letters A–G in the boxes. *Ordne die Satzteile zu und schreibe die richtigen Buchstaben A–G in die Kästchen.*

1 Our small classroom is OK because ...
2 I think geography is great because ...
3 I can't go and see Mr Lee now because ...
4 Liz and Cath aren't my friends because ...
5 I'm not late for my maths lesson because ...
6 It isn't a bad school because ...
7 Our teacher Ms Kemp is tired because ...

A he isn't at school.
B the students and teachers are happy.
C she's always busy.
D it starts in five minutes.
E there aren't a lot of students in our class.
F they aren't very nice.
G it isn't hard.

1 ☐ 2 ☐ 3 ☐ 4 ☐ 5 ☐ 6 ☐ 7 ☐

16 A message from Noah

Complete Noah's message. Use the negative of the verb *be*.
Vervollständige Noahs Nachricht. Verwende die Verneinung des Verbs be.

Hi, Sunita,

I'm in a hotel in London. I (1) ____________ alone here. I'm here with Mum, Dad and Buddy. We (2) ____________ in a very big room, but it's OK. And the food (3) ____________ bad. But I (4) ____________ happy because you (5) ____________ here and because Zane and Lily (6) ____________ here.

See you at school.

Noah

► Check

Der s-Genitiv

Mit dem s-Genitiv drückst du aus, dass etwas zu jemandem gehört.

Singular *(Noah, Mr Lee)*	's	*Noah's dog – Noahs Hund* *Mr Lee's class – Herr Lees Klasse*
Plural mit -s *(boys, Watsons)*	s'	*the boys' phones – die Handys der Jungen* *the Watsons' house – das Haus der Watsons*
Plural ohne -s *(men, women)*	's	*the men's clothes – die Kleidung der Männer* *the women's cars – die Autos der Frauen*

► SB Hello! + Unit 1, p. 202

17 Six sentences and pictures

Write *'s* or *'*. Then match the sentences with the pictures A–F. Write the right letter for each sentence.
Schreibe 's oder '. Ordne dann die Sätze den Bildern A–F zu. Schreibe zu jedem Satz den richtigen Buchstaben.

1 Where's Zane ___ tie? ☐

2 I like the two horses ___ colour. ☐

3 This building ___ windows are very small. ☐

4 I like these people ___ scooters. ☐

5 Those are my friends ___ bikes. ☐

6 I don't like this school ___ uniform. ☐

A

B

C

D

E

F

18 An apostrophe – or not?

Look at sentences 1–6. Put the apostrophe (') in the right place. *Sieh dir die Sätze 1–6 an. Setze ein Apostroph (') an der richtigen Stelle.*

1 Adams dogs are very friendly.

2 My mums favourite colours are pink and grey.

3 The boys names are Tom and George.

4 Ms Smiths opinions aren't helpful.

5 Those are the teachers toilets.

6 The students answers are in the exercise books.

► Check

Die *of*-Fügung

Gehören zwei Sachen zusammen, verbindest du sie mit of.
the end of the story – das Ende der Geschichte

Of verwendest du auch bei Mengenbezeichnungen.
a kilo of oranges – ein Kilo Orangen

▸ SB Hello! + Unit 1, p. 202

19 Words that go together

a) **Complete the phrases with the correct words. Remember to use the word *of*.**
Vervollständige die Ausdrücke mit den richtigen Wörtern. Denke an das Wort of.

1

a ______________________ Brighton

2

a ______________________ apples

3

a ______________________ students

4

a ______________________ the week

5

a ______________________ a book

6

the ______________________ a bike

b) **Read the text. Is the information in the text right or wrong? Tick one box.** *Lies den Text. Sind die Informationen richtig oder falsch? Kreuze an.*

Good to know

Group words in English
In English there are different words for groups of different things or people. We say a class of students, a gang of kids and a team of football players. And for a group of fish? We say a school of fish.

I think this information is right ☐ wrong ☐.

▸ Check

20 REVISION A timetable

Look at Lisa's timetable. Then complete the sentences with the correct form of *be*, positive or negative. *Schau dir Lisas Stundenplan an. Vervollständige die Sätze mit der richtigen Form von* be, *bejaht oder verneint.*

Monday	Tuesday	Wednesday	Thursday	Friday
French	French	geography	English	maths
English	history	maths	maths	French
break	break	break	break	break
science	computing	maths	design and technology	English
science	music	science	history	English
lunch	lunch	lunch	lunch	lunch
computing	art	PE	science	music
design and technology	art	PE	geography	computing

Maths (1) ________________ on Wednesday, Thursday and Friday. English (2) ________________ on Tuesday and Wednesday. It (3) ________________ on Monday, Thursday and Friday. French and computing (4) ________________ on Monday, Tuesday and Friday. They (5) ________________ on Wednesday and Thursday.

Paul It (6) ______________ Tuesday after lunch. You (7) ______________ in your classroom, right, Lisa?

Lisa No, I (8) ______________ in my classroom because I (9) ______________ in the art room.

21 Challenge REVISION Apostrophes

Lisa talks about her school. Read her sentences and put in 15 apostrophes. *Lisa spricht über ihre Schule. Lies ihre Sätze und setze 15 Apostrophe ein.*

Vorsicht! Es gibt Apostrophe in
- *isn't, aren't, ...*
- *my friend's bike, ...*

Its Monday today, so were at school. We arent at the beach. This is my teachers car. It isnt fast. Lets go to my classroom.
The windows in my classroom arent very good.
Oh, Paul and Rufas! Theyre bullies. And the bullies friends arent nice. Theyre mean.
This is my desk and that is our class teachers desk. Oh, this isnt my pen! I think its Bens pen.

► Check

Unit 2
My family and home

Erklär-film

Das Verb *be*: Fragen und Kurzantworten

In Fragen mit *be* verwendest du die Langformen (*long forms*).
Wie im Deutschen steht *be* am Anfang des Satzes, vor dem Subjekt:

You are English. → *Are you English?*   *She is brave.* → *Is she brave?*

Antworte auf eine Frage nicht einfach mit *yes* oder *no*. Das klingt unhöflich. Verwende Kurzantworten.

Fragen	Kurzantworten
Am I right?	Yes, you are. / No, you aren't.
Are you tired?	Yes, I am. / No, I'm not.
	Yes, we are. / No, we aren't.
Is Freya nice?	Yes, she is. / No, she isn't.
Is it late?	Yes, it is. / No, it isn't.
Are Tim and Lisa happy?	Yes, they are. / No, they aren't.

► SB p. 53, p. 206

1 Questions and answers at school

a) Circle the correct form of *be* in the questions. *Kreise in den Fragen die richtige Form von* be *ein.*

1 *Am / Is Mr Lee busy?* — *Yes,* ____________.

2 *Sorry, Sir. Am / Are I late for school?* — *No,* ____________.

3 *Are / Is it Monday today?* — *Yes,* ____________.

4 *Am / Are you OK, Zane?* — *No,* ____________.

5 *Am / Is Sunita tired?* — *No,* ____________.

6 *Are / Is we in room 9 today?* — *Yes,* ____________.

7 *Are / Is Lily and Noah at school today?* — *No,* ____________.

b) Now complete the short answers. *Vervollständige nun die Kurzantworten.*

2 A phone call from Mum

Meg's mum phones to check how things are at home. Complete her questions. Then look at the pictures and write Meg's answers. *Megs Mutter ruft an, um zu sehen, wie die Dinge zu Hause laufen. Vervollständige ihre Fragen. Schau dir dann die Bilder an und schreibe Megs Antworten.*

Überlege, durch welches Personalpronomen du die Personen oder Dinge, um die es in der Frage geht, ersetzen kannst, um die richtige Kurzantwort zu bilden.

1 *______ you at home, Meg?*

______

2 *______ your room messy?*

______

3 *______ your sister happy?*

______

4 *______ your brothers quiet?*

______

5 *______ Dad angry?*

______

6 *And I think you are tired, Meg. ______ I right?*

______

3 Tibbs, my cat

Complete the sentences with the correct form of *be*. *Vervollständige die Sätze mit der richtigen Form von* be.

In Aussagesätzen verwendest du nach Pronomen (*I, you, she, ...*) meist die Kurzform von *be*. Aber: In Fragen und bejahten Kurzantworten verwendest du die Langform.

Tibbs ____________ my cat. But where ____________ Tibbs?

____________ she under my bed? No, she ____________.

Tibbs, where ____________ you?

Maybe she ____________ with our neighbour's cat Moggy. ____________ Tibbs and Moggy in the garden? No, they ____________.

Tibbs, I ____________ angry with you!

____________ I angry with Tibbs? No, I ____________. I can't be angry with Tibbs. She ____________ my cat!

4 Questions and answers

Match the questions 1–6 with the answers A–F.
Ordne die Fragen 1–6 den Antworten A–F zu.

Das Fragewort kommt wie im Deutschen am Anfang des Satzes.
Where am I? – Wo bin ich?
Who are you? – Wer bist du?

1 Where is your house?
2 Who are your neighbours?
3 What is under the table?
4 Who is your class teacher?
5 What are your favourite colours?
6 Where are your mum and dad?

A Yellow and green.
B Ms Patel.
C I think they're with Aunt Jane.
D In Edmund Road.
E Mike and Rowena.
F My cat.

There is ... / There are ...

Mit *there is* (*there's*) und *there are* sagst du, dass etwas vorhanden ist. Im Deutschen heißt es meist: Es gibt ..., Da sind ..., Es stehen ..., Da liegen ...

Du verwendest:

- There's ... mit dem Singular
  There's a cat in our kitchen. – Da ist eine Katze in unserer Küche.
  Is there a toilet here? – Yes, there is. – Gibt es hier eine Toilette? – Ja.
- There are ... mit dem Plural
  There are three bedrooms in our flat. – Es gibt drei Schlafzimmer in unserer Wohnung.
  Are there lots of people here? – Yes, there are. – Gibt es hier viele Menschen? – Ja.

► SB p. 56, p. 206

5 What's in the garden?

a) **Look at the picture. Complete the sentences with *There's* or *There are* and the correct words.** *Schau dir das Bild an. Vervollständige die Sätze mit* There's *oder* There are *und den richtigen Wörtern.*

1 ______________ two nice big *trees* ______________ (TEERS) in the garden.

2 ______________ four ______________ (POEPEL) in the garden: two boys and two girls.

3 ______________ two ______________ (AMANILS): two cats.

4 ______________ a brown ______________ (TALEB).

5 ______________ a black and white ______________ (FOTOBLAL).

6 ______________ a yellow ______________ (BEKI).

b) **Now complete the questions and answers.** *Vervollständige nun die Fragen und Antworten.*

1 ______________ there a cat in the garden? Yes, there ______________.

2 ______________ there some chairs in the garden? Yes, there ______________.

3 ______________ there a lot of rabbits in the garden? No, ______________.

4 ______________ there a hamster in the garden? No, ______________.

Die Possessivbegleiter

Possessivbegleiter zeigen an, wem etwas gehört.

I	→	*my sister – meine Schwester*	we	→	*our kitchen – unsere Küche*
you	→	*your house – dein Haus*	you	→	*your car – euer Auto*
he	→	*his clothes – seine Kleider*	they	→	*their bedroom – ihr Schlafzimmer*
she	→	*her laptop – ihr Laptop*			
it	→	*its colour – seine/ihre Farbe*			

!

- it's = it is: *It's cold today. – Es ist kalt heute.*
  its = sein, ihr: *our garden with its trees – unser Garten mit seinen Bäumen*
- they're = *they are: They're German. – Sie sind Deutsche.*
  Their = ihr(e): *Here are Dan and Jo with their dad. – Hier sind Dan und Jo mit ihrem Vater.*

▸ SB Units 1–2, p. 204

6 Photos

Sunita shows Noah some photos. (Circle) the correct words. *Sunita zeigt Noah Fotos. Kreise die richtigen Wörter ein.*

1 Look! That's my / our / his brother and our / their / her parrot George.

2 And that's me in my / her / their room.

3 And there are my / his / their mum and Ben in our / his / their bedroom.

4 There's Willow with her / his / our new phone.

5 And that's you, Noah, with my / your / her dog!

6 There are her / our / my neighbours in their / his / her garden.

7 Sunita's family

Complete the sentences with the words from the box.
Vervollständige die Sätze mit den Wörtern aus dem Kasten.

her • his • its • my • our • their • your

Noah Is all (1) ____________ family in Brighton, Sunita?

Sunita Well, Mum, Nish and I are in Brighton. (2) ____________ house is in Palmeira Road. Mum is a vet and there are animals from (3) ____________ work in our house. And there's Mum's partner Ben with (4) ____________ daughter Willow. They're in Brighton too. But Aunt Priya, Uncle Rahi, Jay and Neeta live in Birmingham. Jay and Neeta are (5) ____________ cousins. I really like (6) ____________ house with (7) ____________ nice big garden. Mum's parents live in India.

8 At Sunita's house

Noah is at Sunita's house. Complete his sentences with *it's* or *its*. *Noah ist in Sunitas Haus. Vervollständige seine Sätze mit* it's *oder* its.

I really like your house with (1) ______________ nice big garden. There are a lot of trees here. (2) ______________ nice. Wow! And I like your room! (3) ______________ really cool. And I like your sofa with (4) ______________ nice cushions! I like your parrot and I like (5) ______________ name too. Oh look, (6) ______________ late. Time to go home.

☒ 9 REVISION Khaled's new house

Complete the conversation with the correct words from the box. *Vervollständige die Unterhaltung mit den richtigen Wörtern aus dem Kasten.*

am • are • aren't • her • is • its • it's • my • their • there • they • they're • ~~your~~

Dan Are you in (1) *your* ______________ new house, Khaled?

Khaled Yes, Dan, I (2) ______________.

Dan And (3) ______________ it nice?

Khaled Yes, it is. (4) ______________ really nice. My sister is lucky because (5) ______________ bedroom is nice and big. But I'm happy too because I have (6) ______________ own room with a bed, of course, a wardrobe and a desk. Oh, and some shelves. (7) ______________ next to my bed.

Dan And are your school friends near you?

Khaled No, they (8) ______________. But (9) ______________ are other nice kids here.

Dan And what about your neighbours. (10) ______________ they nice?

Khaled Yes, (11) ______________ are. And (12) ______________ dog is really cute. (13) ______________ name is Melanie. You must come and see me here, Dan!

Unit 3
My day

Erklär-film

Das simple present

Mit dem *simple present* sagst du, was oft, jeden Tag oder nie passiert.

I / you / we / they play
he / she/ it / my sister plays   ! *He, she* und *it*, das -*s* muss mit!

Häufige Signalwörter im *simple present* sind: *always* (immer), *often* (oft), *sometimes* (manchmal), *rarely* (selten), *never* (nie).

► SB p. 88, p. 207

1 Sunita's school day

a) **Read Sunita's text. <u>Underline</u> the signal words for the simple present.** *Lies Sunitas Text. Unterstreiche die Signalwörter für das simple present.*

b) **Highlight the verbs that end in -*s* in the 3rd person simple present.** *Markiere die Verben, die auf -s enden (3. Person Singular im simple present).*

I always get up at 6.15. School starts at 8.45, so I get the bus at 8.15, or my mum sometimes takes me by car.

I like science and design and technology, but I often find art quite hard. I rarely draw nice pictures. But Lily often draws very cool pictures.

I never come home for lunch – I always eat at school.

School ends at 2.55 and I come home by bus.

We have dinner at six o'clock and I rarely go to bed before nine o'clock.

2 Sunita and Willow

Complete Sunita's sentences. Then complete the sentences about Willow.
Vervollständige Sunitas Sätze. Vervollständige dann die Sätze über Willow.

eat • get • find • like

1 I __________ up at 6.15.
2 I __________ science.
3 I __________ art quite hard.
4 I always __________ at school.

A Willow __________ up at 7.00.
B Willow __________ maths.
C She __________ English quite hard.
D She always __________ at school too.

► Check

3 Crossword

a) **Fill the crossword with the correct verbs in the simple present.** *Vervollständige das Kreuzworträtsel mit den richtigen Verben im simple present.*

My friend Karina ...

My friend Jason ... to music.

My dad ... on Sundays.

I ... my friends in town.

My friends Dan and Eli ... stories.

I often ... my friends.

My mum ... to her work.

My sister ... the guitar.

My brother ... in a club at school

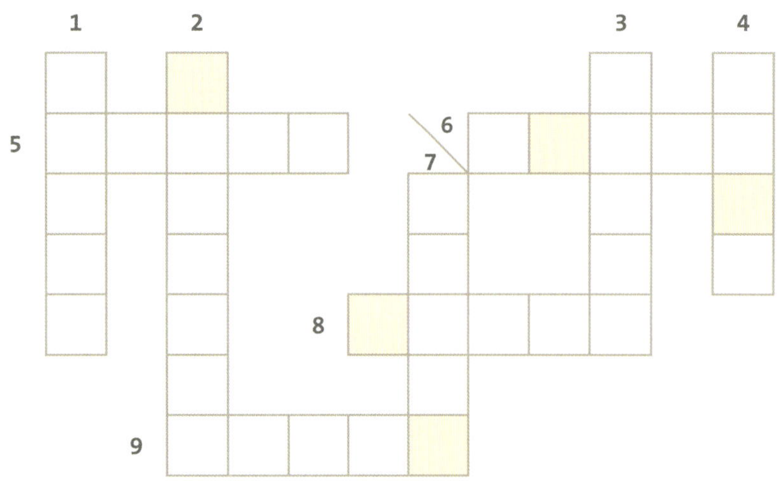

b) **The highlighted letters in a make a word. Write it.**
Die markierten Buchstaben in a ergeben ein Wort. Schreibe es.

Zane always ______________________________ his mum at home.

► Check

4 My brother Isaac

Add -*s* to the simple present form of the verbs if necessary. *Ergänze -s am Ende des Verbs, wo nötig.*

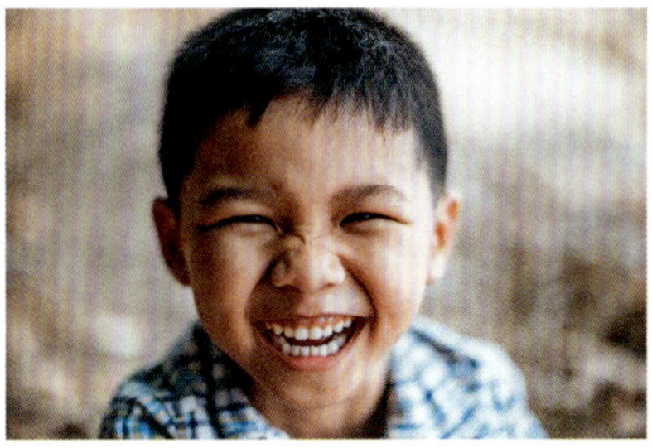

I love______ my brother Isaac. He's only four years old, but he love ______ books, so I often read______ to him when I come______ home from school. He really like______ that and he often ask______ a lot of questions. He often draw ______ pictures or dream______ when I read ______ to him. At the end of a story we often talk______ about the book and then Isaac tell______ our parents all about the story when we eat______ in the evening. And he remember______ everything!

5 My week

Write sentences in the simple present. *Schreibe Sätze im simple present.*

1 Mondays – I – always – play football

On Mondays I always ____________________

2 Tuesdays – my sister – often – go swimming

____

3 Wednesdays – Dad – never – come home – before 8 p.m.

____

4 Thursdays – Mum – often – go – to yoga

____

5 Fridays – we – always – eat fish – for dinner

____

6 Saturdays – Grandpa – often – visit us

____

7 Sundays – I – never – get up – before 10 a.m.

____

▸ Check

Das simple present: Sonderformen

Es gibt im *simple present* ein paar Sonderformen bei *he/she/it*:

- An Verben, die auf -ss, -x, -sh, -ch oder -o enden, hängst du (statt -s) -es an:

  brush: He brushes his teeth. *watch: My sister watches TV.*

  go: She goes to school. *do: My dad does parkour.*

- Bei Verben, die auf Konsonant + -y enden, wird -y bei *he/she/it* zu -ies: *tidy: My brother tidies his room.*
- Das Verb have hat bei *he/she/it* die Form has: *Our flat has three bedrooms.*

► SB p. 88, p. 207

6 Students in Toyin's class

Complete the sentences with the simple present of the verbs in the box. *Vervollständige die Sätze mit dem simple present der Verben im Kasten.*

brush • bully • do • go • have • tidy • watch

1 Emma is a rugby fan and ______________________ all the big rugby matches on TV.

2 Ravi ______________________ a really nice big dog. He ______________________ it every day.

3 Layla always ______________________ her desk at the end of the school day.

4 I don't like Tim. He often ______________________ other students.

5 Mel sometimes ______________________ to an old people's home and ______________________ a lot for the people there.

7 Toyin and her sister

Write the verbs in the simple present. *Schreibe die Verben im simple present.*

My sister and I ______________________ (1 have) very different hobbies. I'm a football fan and I ______________________ (2 play) in a club in town. My sister sometimes ______________________ (3 come) to the club too and ______________________ (4 watch) us. My sister ______________________ (5 have) dancing lessons. She always ______________________ (6 go) to her dancing lesson on Tuesdays. She ______________________ (7 do) some really nice dancing moves!

► Check

Die Wortstellung

In Aussagesätzen ist die Wortstellung: subject – verb – object.

Dad	*makes*	*dinner*	when	*he*	*comes*	*home from work*
Papa	*macht*	*das Abendessen,*	wenn	*er*	*von der Arbeit nach Hause*	*kommt.*

Mit Häufigkeitsadverbien (*always, often, sometimes, rarely, never*) kannst du sagen, wie oft etwas geschieht. Anders als im Deutschen stehen sie im Englischen meist direkt vor dem Hauptverb.

We sometimes play a game. – Wir spielen manchmal ein Spiel.

▸ SB p. 91, p. 207

8 The right order

Look at the diagram. Write the right word in each line. *Schaue dir das Diagramm an. Schreibe das richtige Wort in jede Zeile.*

always • never • often • rarely • sometimes

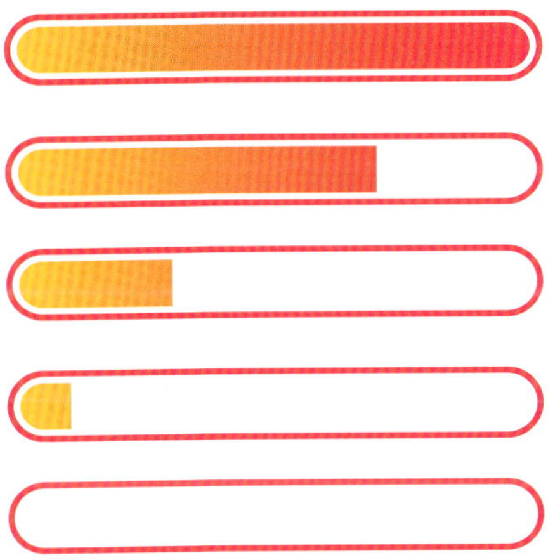

1 ______________________

2 ______________________

3 ______________________

4 ______________________

5 ______________________

9 Cooking club

Write sentences. Put the words in the right order. *Schreibe Sätze. Bringe die Wörter in die richtige Reihenfolge.*

1 We / on Wednesday after school / always / meet

We ______________________

2 meet / sometimes / on Saturday morning / And we

And we ______________________

3 We / nice food / cook / often

____

4 never / have / we / a bad time

____

▸ Check

10 You're the teacher!

Here's an article about sport in German schools. But there are five mistakes in it. First correct the article with arrows. Then complete the corrected text. *Hier ist ein Artikel über Sport an deutschen Schulen. Allerdings haben sich fünf Fehler eingeschlichen. Markiere zuerst die Fehler mit Pfeilen. Vervollständige dann den korrigierten Text.*

Sport in German schools

In German schools we play never cricket. We play often handball and basketball. We play often football in clubs in town because schools rarely place to play football have. But I think schools in Germany have always a sports hall.

In German schools ______

______

______ and basketball.

______

______

______

______ But I think ______

______

______

11 Mediation

You and your class visit a school in England and talk to the English students. Help your German friend with her sentences. *Du und deine Klasse besucht eine Schule in England und ihr unterhaltet euch mit den englischen Schülerinnen und Schülern. Hilf deiner Freundin bei ihren Sätzen.*

1 *Wir fahren oft in die Stadt.*

2 *Aber wir fahren selten mit dem Auto.*

3 *Ich fahre oft mit dem Fahrrad.*

4 *Mein Bruder fährt manchmal mit dem Zug.*

5 *Aber wir gehen nie zu Fuß in die Stadt.*

1 We ______

2 But we ______

3 ______

4 ______
______

5 ______
______

► Check

ADVANCED

lighthouse 1

Grammarmaster

Lösungen

Cornelsen

Unit 1 My new school

Alle Lösungen aus diesem Heft findest du auch in deiner Cornelsen Lernen App.

1 T-shirts

a)

1 a lion
2 a horse
3 an elephant
4 a seagull
5 an apple
6 an orange
7 a hat
8 a bike

b)

1 **A** horse is **an** animal. **An** elephant is **an** animal too.
2 You can eat **an** apple. But you can't eat **a** glue stick! Yuk!
3 I can see **a** zebra, **a** gorilla and **an** orang utan.

2 At school

1 I have **a** book. It's **a** big book. It's **an** English book.
2 And I have **a** pencil. It's **an** old pencil, but I like it.
3 I have **an** exercise book. It's **an** orange exercise book.
4 We have **a** uniform. It's **a** blue and grey uniform.
5 'My new school' is **a** unit in my English book. It's **a** good unit.

3 Mr Lee's sentences

a) b)

		ðə	ði	ðə	ði
1	Look at the **b**oard!	✓			
2	Open the **b**ook at page 21.	✓			
3	Eat the **a**pple, please.		✓		
4	Listen to the **m**usic and to the **E**nglish students.	✓			✓
5	Look at the **p**icture of the **o**ld horse.	✓			✓

4 Sunita is at the zoo

I can see two **elephants**, three **men**, four **women**, five **snakes**, six **lions**, seven **children** and eight **parrots**.

5 Words with -y

a) b)

1 holid**a**y – holidays
2 hob**b**y – hobbies
3 monk**e**y – monkeys
4 po**n**y – ponies

6 More than one

a) b)

1 friend: **1** – Hassan and Sasha are my **friends**.
2 baby: **3** – I love **babies**.
3 box: **2** – Look at the words in the two **boxes**.
4 sandwich: **2** – I eat **sandwiches** at school.
5 pen, pencil: **1** – I have two **pens** and three **pencils** in my pencil case.
6 party: **3** – **Parties** are great!

7 My new school

1 I have a new timetable. **It** is OK.
2 My class teacher is Ms Ahmed. **She** is nice.
3 My friends and I are in the same class. **We** are in 7B.
4 Max is a student in my class. **He** is from Oxford.
5 Look! Livvy and Dan are very tired. **They** are asleep.

8 At school

1 She's great.
2 It's blue and grey.
3 Here it is.
4 He's in the classroom.
5 They're in room 11.
6 Yes, I have my uniform and my school bag.
7 We're four good friends.

☒ 9 Sunita, Lily, Noah and Zane at school

1 you • **2** I • **3** I • **4** they • **5** you • **6** I • **7** I • **8** I / We • **9** it • **10** It • **11** You • **12** You • **13** I • **14** he • **15** you / we • **16** We • **17** we

10 Where are you from?

1 Where are you from, Milo and Oliver? – We**'re** from Brighton.
2 And you**'re** from Brighton too, right, Ivy? – No, I**'m** from Leeds.
3 And where is Zahra from? – She**'s** from London.
4 Where are Lin and Kiera from? – They**'re** from Oxford.
5 Where is Jason from? – He**'s** from Manchester.

11 Class 7C

1 Sarah and I **are** in 7C.
2 But all my other friends **are** all in 7K.
3 My maths teacher **is** Ms Khan.
4 Art and PE **are** two subjects at my school.
5 Assembly **is** on Tuesday and Thursday.
6 The timetable **is** OK.

12 Class 7K

1 They're nice.
2 We're 25 students in 7K.
3 She's nice.
4 He's from London.
5 I'm happy in my class.
6 You're welcome, Mia!

13 Two messages

a)

Hi Nazim. I**'m** in London with Dad. It**'s** nice here. We**'re** in London Zoo. I like the monkeys. They**'re** great! See you soon. Kinga

Hi, Kinga. You**'re** lucky. I**'m** in Brighton and I can't go swimming with Mum. She**'s** tired. And I can't play basketball with Lily and Zane. They**'re** busy.

b)

1 Kinga **is** lucky.
2 She and her dad **are** in London Zoo.
3 It **is** nice there.
4 The monkeys **are** great.
5 But Nazim **is** in Brighton and his mum **is** tired.
6 And Lily and Zane **are** busy.

14 Nice or not nice?

1 We **aren't** busy.
2 Parkour **isn't** hard.
3 I**'m not** lucky!
4 The cats **aren't** very happy!
5 Nav **isn't** good at yoga.
6 It **isn't** great here!

15 At school

1 E • **2** G • **3** A • **4** F • **5** D • **6** B • **7** C

16 A message from Noah

Hi, Sunita, I'm in a hotel in London. **I'm not** alone here. I'm here with Mum, Dad and Buddy. We **aren't** in a very big room, but it's OK. And the food **isn't** bad. But **I'm not** happy because you **aren't** here and because Zane and Lily **aren't** here. See you at school. Noah

17 Six sentences and pictures

1 Where's Zane**'s** tie? **C**
2 I like the two horses' colour. **E**
3 This building**'s** windows are very small. **B**
4 I like these people**'s** scooters. **F**
5 Those are my friends' bikes. **D**
6 I don't like this school**'s** uniform. **A**

18 An apostrophe – or not?

1 Adam's dogs are very friendly.
2 My mum's favourite colours are pink and grey.
3 The boys' names are Tom and George.
4 Ms Smith's opinions aren't helpful.
5 Those are the teachers' toilets.
6 The students' answers are in the exercise books.

19 Words that go together

a)

1 a map of Brighton
2 a bag of apples
3 a class of students
4 a day of the week
5 a page of a book
6 the chain of a bike

b)

The information is right.

20 REVISION A timetable

1 is
2 isn't
3 's
4 are
5 aren't
6 's
7 're
8 'm not
9 'm

21 Challenge REVISION Apostrophes

It's Monday today, so we're at school. We aren't at the beach. This is my teacher's car. It isn't fast.
Let's go to my classroom.
The windows in my classroom aren't very good.
Oh, Paul and Rufas! They're bullies. And the bullies' friends aren't nice. They're mean.
This is my desk and that is our class teacher's desk. Oh, this isn't my pen! I think it's Ben's pen.

Unit 2 My family and home

1 Questions and answers at school

a) b)

1 **Is** Mr Lee busy? – Yes, **he is**.
2 Sorry, Sir. **Am** I late for school? – No, **you aren't**.
3 **Is** it Monday today? – Yes, **it is**.
4 **Are** you OK, Zane? – No, **I'm not**.
5 **Is** Sunita tired? – No, **she isn't**.
6 **Are** we in room 9 today? – Yes, **we are**.
7 **Are** Lily and Noah at school today? – No, **they aren't**.

2 A phone call from Mum

1 **Are** you at home, Meg? – **Yes, I am.**
2 **Is** your room messy? – **No, it isn't.**
3 **Is** your sister happy? – **Yes, she is.**
4 **Are** your brothers quiet? – **No, they aren't.**
5 **Is** Dad angry? – **Yes, he is.**
6 And I think you are tired, Meg. **Am** I right? – **Yes, you are.**

3 Tibbs, my cat

1 Tibbs **is** my cat. But where **is** Tibbs?
2 **Is** she under my bed? No, she **isn't**.
3 Tibbs, where **are** you?
4 Maybe she**'s** with our neighbour's cat Moggy. **Are** Tibbs and Moggy in the garden? No, they **aren't**.
5 Tibbs, I**'m** angry with you!
6 **Am** I angry with Tibbs? No, I**'m not**. I can't be angry with Tibbs. She**'s** my cat!

4 Questions and answers

1 D • **2** E • **3** F • **4** B • **5** A • **6** C

5 What's in the garden?

a)
1 **There are** two nice big **trees** in the garden.
2 **There are** four **people** in the garden: two boys and two girls.
3 **There are** two **animals**: two cats.
4 **There's** a brown **table**.
5 **There's** a black and white **football**.
6 **There's** a yellow **bike**.

b)
1 **Is** there a cat in the garden? Yes, there **is**.
2 **Are** there some chairs in the garden? Yes, there **are**.
3 **Are** there a lot of rabbits in the garden? No, **there aren't**.
4 **Is** there a hamster in the garden? No, **there isn't**.

6 Photos

1 Look! That's **my** brother and **our** parrot George.
2 And that's me in **my** room.
3 And there are **my** mum and Ben in **their** bedroom.
4 There's Willow with **her** new phone.
5 And that's you, Noah, with **your** dog!
6 There are **our** neighbours in **their** garden.

7 Sunita's family

1 your
2 Our
3 her
4 his
5 my
6 their
7 its

8 At Sunita's house

1 its
2 It's
3 It's
4 its
5 its
6 it's

9 Revision Khaled's new house

1 your • **2** am • **3** is • **4** It's • **5** her • **6** my • **7** They're • **8** aren't • **9** there • **10** Are • **11** they • **12** their • **13** Its

Unit 3 My day

1 Sunita's school day

a) b)

I always get up at 6.15. School starts at 8.45, so I get the bus at 8.15, or my mum sometimes takes me by car.
I like science and design and technology, but I often find art quite hard. I rarely draw nice pictures. But Lily often draws very cool pictures.
I never come home for lunch – I always eat at school.
School ends at 2.55 and I come home by bus.
We have dinner at six o'clock and I rarely go to bed before nine o'clock.

2 Sunita and Willow

1 I **get up** at 6.15.
2 I **like** science.
3 I **find** art quite hard.
4 I always **eat** at school.

A Willow **gets up** at 7.00.
B Willow **likes** maths.
C She **finds** English quite hard.
D She always **eats** at school too.

3 Crossword

a)

	1		2							3		4
	S		L							C		M
5	W	R	I	T	E		6 / 7	P	H	O	N	E
	I		S				W			O		E
	M		T				A			K		T
	S		E		8	P	L	A	Y	S		
			N				K					
		9	S	I	N	G	S					

b)

Zane always **helps** his mum at home.

4 My brother Isaac

I love my brother Isaac. He's only four years old, but he love**s** books, so I often read to him when I come home from school. He really like**s** that and he often ask**s** a lot of questions. He often draw**s** pictures or dream**s** when I read to him. At the end of a story we often talk about the book and then Isaac tell**s** our parents all about the story when we eat in the evening. And he remember**s** everything!

5 My week
1 On Mondays I always play football.
2 On Tuesdays my sister often goes swimming.
3 On Wednesdays Dad never comes home before 8 p.m.
4 On Thursdays Mum often goes to yoga.
5 On Fridays we always eat fish for dinner.
6 On Saturdays Grandpa often visits us.
7 On Sundays I never get up before 10 a.m.

6 Students in Toyin's class
1 Emma is a rugby fan and **watches** all the big rugby matches on TV.
2 Ravi **has** a really nice big dog. He **brushes** it every day.
3 Layla always **tidies** her desk at the end of the school day.
4 I don't like Tim. He often **bullies** other students.
5 Mel sometimes **goes** to an old people's home and **does** a lot for the people there.

7 Toyin and her sister
My sister and I **have** very different hobbies. I'm a football fan and I **play** in a club in town. My sister sometimes **comes** to the club too and **watches** us.
My sister **has** dancing lessons. She always **goes** to her dancing lesson on Tuesdays. She **does** some really nice dancing moves!

8 The right order
1 always
2 often
3 sometimes
4 rarely
5 never

9 Cooking club
1 We always meet on Wednesday after school.
2 And we sometimes meet on Saturday morning.
3 We often cook nice food.
4 We never have a bad time.

10 You're the teacher!
In German schools we **never play** cricket. We **often play** handball and basketball. We **often play** football in clubs in town because schools rarely **have** place to play football. But I think schools in Germany **always have** a sports hall.

11 Mediation
1 We often go to town.
2 But we rarely go by car.
3 I often go by bike.
4 My brother sometimes goes by train.
5 But we never walk to town.

12 Revision Quiz: Who is it?

a)

1 He cook**s** food for his family. He**'s** a good swimmer. His mum use**s** a wheelchair. He take**s** his sister to her school. **Zane**

2 She go**es** to school by bus. She like**s** computers and she often do**es** coding. She help**s** Noah when Jade bull**ies** him. **Sunita**

b)

3 This boy **goes** to school by car. He **has** a dog, Buddy. He really **likes** his dog. He (the boy, not the dog!) **is** always hungry. **Noah**

c)

4 She often does parkour. **Lily**

5 He's often tired because **he always works long days in a cafe.** **Eno / Zane's dad**

Unit 4 Where I live

1 East Dean

a)

My grandparents live in East Dean. East Dean is about 25 kilometres from Brighton. It's a small place and it doesn't have big estates. It isn't next to the sea, so it doesn't have a pier or a marina. And it doesn't have a cinema. The children of East Dean don't go to school there: they go to school in Eastbourne. My grandparents don't work there because they work in Eastbourne too. So East Dean doesn't have much, but the people there are very friendly. My brother and sister don't like East Dean. They say it's boring because it doesn't have a sports centre. But I like East Dean because my grandparents live there.

b)

1 My grandparents **don't** watch films in East Dean because it **doesn't** have a cinema.
2 Young people **don't** go to school in East Dean because it **doesn't** have a secondary school.
3 East Dean **doesn't** have many places and my grandparents **don't** work there.
4 East Dean **doesn't** have rubbish in its streets. Why? I **don't** know why.

2 The lost bag

1 don't
2 don't
3 don't
4 doesn't
5 don't
6 doesn't
7 don't
8 don't
9 don't
10 doesn't

3 Zane and Noah are different

1 Zane gets up at 7 a.m., but Noah doesn't **get up** at 7 a.m.
2 Zane walks to school, but Noah **doesn't walk to school.**
3 Zane has a sister, Holly, but **Noah doesn't have a sister.**
4 Zane takes Holly to school, but **Noah doesn't take Holly to school.**
5 Zane goes swimming, but **Noah doesn't go swimming.**
6 Zane watches TV in the evening, but **Noah doesn't watch TV in the evening.**

4 Likes and dislikes

1 Hi, I'm Ollie. I have a cat. I don't have a dog.
2 My sister plays football. She doesn't play table tennis.
3 We live in a flat. We don't live in a house.
4 My parents like fish and chips. They don't like soup.
5 Mum does yoga. She doesn't do parkour.
6 Our neighbour has a bike. He doesn't have a car.

5 Some students in my class

1 Radhia and Diya don't live on my estate.
2 Kiera doesn't go to the youth centre.
3 Max reads books in the library.
4 Cindy doesn't cook for her family.
5 Luca does skateboarding.

6 Zara's new flat

1 doesn't have
2 has
3 have
4 don't share
5 don't walk
6 use
7 doesn't put
8 put
9 watches
10 come
11 doesn't say
12 thinks

7 Questions for you

1 Yes, I do. / No, I don't
2 Yes, it does. / No, it doesn't.
3 Yes, I do. / No, I don't.
4 Yes, it does. / No, it doesn't.

8 Can you remember?

a)
1 **Do** Lily and her parents live on an estate? – **Yes**, they **do**.
2 **Does** Lily's estate have some problems? – **Yes**, it **does**.
3 **Does** Lily live with her sister? – **No**, she **doesn't**.
4 **Do** Lily and her parents have a car? – **No**, they **don't**.
5 **Does** Lily's dad sometimes go walking with Lily? – **Yes**, he **does**.

9 Saturday activities

1 **Does** Grace go to the pier on Saturdays? – Yes, **she does.**
2 **Do** Sam and Jo go shopping in the Lanes on Saturdays? – **Yes, they do.**
3 **Do** Mr and Mrs Jones go to Jubilee Library on Saturdays? – No, **they don't.**
4 **Does** Milan go to the Brighton i360 on Saturdays? – **Yes, he does.**
5 **Does** Hannah go to St. Nicholas Rest Garden on Saturdays? – **No, she doesn't.**
6 **Do** Phil and his friends go to the station on Saturdays? – **No, they don't.**
7 **Does** Norah go to the museum on Saturdays? – **Yes, she does.**
8 **Do** Amy and her dad go to the shopping centre on Saturdays? – **Yes, they do.**

10 Questions about school

a) b)

1 How do you go to school? – By bus.
2 When does your first lesson start? – At 8.50 a.m.
3 Where do you have lunch? – In the canteen.
4 What do you do in your lunch break? – I talk with my friends.

11 More questions about school

1 What do you bring to school?
2 ✓
3 What do you have for lunch?
4 ✓

12 REVISION Brighton beach

1 is
2 have
3 swims
4 go
5 reads
6 does
7 listen
8 go
9 buys
10 closes
11 want
12 goes

13 REVISION At Hove Skatepark

1 I don't like skateboarding.
2 I can't skateboard very well.
3 Skateboarding isn't fun!
4 My skateboard doesn't work well!

14 REVISION Weekends

1 do you like
2 don't know
3 doesn't want
4 wants
5 go
6 do you do
7 cook
8 like
9 cooks
10 don't cook

☒ 15 REVISION Too many questions about the pier

Tourist **Is** it free to go on the pier?
Zane Yes, it is.
Tourist **Are there** trampolines?
Zane Yes, there are.
Tourist **Do** they **have** special activities at Halloween?
Zane Yes, they do. They have special activities at Halloween and also at Christmas.
Tourist **Can** you buy fish and chips on the pier?
Zane Yes, you can.
Tourist And when **does** the pier **close**?
Zane It closes at 6 p.m.
Tourist Thank you. But it's cloudy and windy. I think it's too cold for the pier today!

Unit 5 Enjoy!

1 Noah's visit to London Zoo

a)
1 I'**m** taking lots of photos today.
2 Listen! The parrots **are** making a lot of noise!
3 That big tiger **is** watching me!
4 All the visitors **are** enjoying the sun.

b)
1 'm visiting
2 're walking
3 're standing
4 's eating
5 'm really enjoying

2 Three activities

1 Look! Jody and Mark **are making** a trifle! They**'re putting** strawberries on it.
2 Jo **is looking** happy. She**'s smiling** because her mum **is decorating** her birthday cake.
3 I**'m eating** an Indian dish, matter paneer. And my friend Kabir **is writing** the recipe for me.

3 Double letters

1 ru**nn**ing
2 wi**nn**ing
3 swi**mm**ing
4 si**tt**ing
5 sto**pp**ing
6 ge**tt**ing

4 Meera and Ben are away one weekend

a)
1 Sunita and Nish aren't **cleaning the kitchen.**
2 The dishwasher **isn't working.**
3 I'm so worried about Sunita and Nish that I**'m not sleeping.**

b)
1 Are you and Nish enjoying the weekend alone?
2 Are George and the other animals eating their food?
3 Are you tidying the house?
4 Am I texting too often?

☒ ## 5 A birthday party

1 **Are** the girls **having** a birthday party? – Yes, they **are**.
2 **Is** it **raining**? – **No, it isn't.**
3 **Are** the girls **smiling**? – **Yes, they are.**
4 **Are** they **wearing** birthday hats? – **No, they aren't.**
5 **Are** the girls **singing**? – **No, they aren't.**
6 **Is** one girl **eating**? – **Yes, it is.**

6 And you?

b) ((Lösungsbeispiel))
I'm sitting at my desk at home.
I'm doing my homework.
My mum is working in our garden.
I'm feeling happy because it's the weekend.

7 Much or many?

How much ...?	How many ...?
flour	*bikes*
fruit	*ballons*
money	*men*
love	*people*
time	*oranges*

8 Questions about school

1 By bus. But there aren't **many** buses from our estate to town. There are usually **a lot of** people on the bus, so I usually stand.
2 The food isn't bad, but I think the problem is that we don't get **much** time to eat it. **A lot of** students need to use the canteen and it isn't very big.
3 It's OK. We often don't get **much** homework. That's good because my brothers are at home and there's often **a lot of** noise.
4 We do **a lot of** different sports at school and I enjoy it. But we don't do **many** different sorts of athletics.
5 Usually yes. I have **a lot of** friends. I think it's maybe hard for students who don't have **many** friends.

9 Quiz

1 How **many** players are there in a rugby team? B fifteen
2 How **much** food does an elephant eat in a day? B 150 to 160 kilos
3 How **much** rain does London get? A about the same as Paris
4 How **many** colours must a trifle have? B three: red jelly, yellow custard and white cream
5 How **many** people live in Britain? A over 65 million
6 How **much** time can a game of cricket take? B three to five days

10 Our town

1 a lot of
2 many
3 a lof of / many
4 many
5 much
6 much
7 many
8 much

11 Lily and Zane's picnic

a) b)

1 **Zane** How many eggs do we have?
Lily There aren't many eggs.
2 **Zane** How much ham do we have?
Lily There isn't much ham.
3 **Zane** How much cheese do we have?
Lily There's a lot of cheese.
4 **Zane** How many carrots do we have?
Lily There aren't many carrots.
5 **Zane** How much bread do we have?
Lily There's a lot of bread.
6 **Zane** How many sausages do we have?
Lily There aren't many sausages.

12 What you do

((Lösungsbeispiel))
I don't eat much honey.
I eat a lot of Chinese food.
I don't eat many bananas.
I drink a lot of water.
I drink a lot of tea too.
I don't drink much lemonade.

13 Challenge REVISION Holiday messages from Wales

a)

1 Present progressive, weil Chris gerade jetzt in Wales ist.
2 Simple present, weil das Fahrradfahren regelmäßig (jeden Tag) passiert.
3 Present progressive, weil es gerade jetzt passiert.

b) c)

Hi from Wales! We usually **visit** places in England in our holidays, but this year we**'re visiting** some friends in Wales. Most days we **go** to the beach and **swim** in the sea. It's quite cold, but OK. But today is different. It**'s raining** today, so we're at home. I**'m texting** my friends, dad **is cooking** and mum and Bridget **are playing** cards. They always **play** cards when they can. Are you at home this week? I hope you**'re having** a good time. Say hi to your family from me.

12 Revision Quiz: Who is it?

a) **Complete the sentences with *-s, -es, -'s* or *-ies*. Then write who it is.** *Vervollständige die Sätze mit* -s, -es, -'s *oder* -ies. *Schreibe dann den Namen der gesuchten Person.*

1 He cook ________ food for his family. He ________ a good swimmer. His mum use ________ a wheelchair. He take ________ his sister to her school.

____

2 She go ________ to school by bus. She like ________ computers and she often do ________ coding. She help ________ Noah when Jade bull ________ him.

____

b) **Complete the sentences with the missing words. Then write who it is.** *Vervollständige die Sätze mit den fehlenden Wörtern. Schreibe dann den Namen der gesuchten Person.*

3 This boy ____________ to school by car. He ____________ a dog, Buddy. He really ____________ his dog. He (the boy, not the dog!) ____________ always hungry.

____

c) **Write sentences. Put the words in the right order. Then write who it is.** *Schreibe Sätze. Bringe die Wörter in die richtige Reihenfolge. Schreibe dann den Namen der gesuchten Person.*

4 often / parkour / does / she

____

____

5 long days in a cafe / always / works / he

He's often tired because ________________________________

____

____

▸ Check

Unit 4
Where I live

Das simple present: Verneinte Aussagesätze

Um Aussagen im *simple present* zu verneinen, verwendest du don't oder doesn't.

I you we they my parents	+ don't + verb	he she it my brother	+ doesn't + verb

I don't like maths. – Ich mag Mathe nicht.
My mum doesn't work in town. – Meine Mutter arbeitet nicht in der Stadt.
We don't play cricket. – Wir spielen nicht Cricket.

► SB p. 119, p. 208

1 East Dean

a) **A student writes an article about the place where his grandparents live. Read the text. Highlight the verbs in the negative.** *Ein Schüler schreibt einen Artikel über den Ort, an dem seine Großeltern leben. Lies den Artikel. Markiere alle verneinten Verben.*

www.eastdean.example.com

My grandparents live in East Dean. East Dean is about 25 kilometres from Brighton. It's a small place and it doesn't have big estates. It isn't next to the sea, so it doesn't have a pier or a marina. And it doesn't have a cinema. The children of East Dean don't go to school there: they go to school in Eastbourne. My grandparents don't work there because they work in Eastbourne too. So East Dean doesn't have much, but the people there are very friendly. My brother and sister don't like East Dean. They say it's boring because it doesn't have a sports centre. But I like East Dean because my grandparents live there.

b) **Circle the correct form: *doesn't* or *don't*.** *Kreise die richtige Form ein:* doesn't *oder* don't.

1 My grandparents doesn't / don't watch films in East Dean because it doesn't / don't have a cinema.

2 Young people doesn't / don't go to school in East Dean because it doesn't / don't have a secondary school.

3 East Dean doesn't / don't have many places and my grandparents doesn't / don't work there.

4 East Dean doesn't / don't have rubbish in its streets. Why? I doesn't / don't know why.

► Check

2 The lost bag

Complete the sentences with *don't* or *doesn't*. *Vervollständige die Sätze mit* don't *oder* doesn't.

Sunita Where's my bag? I (1) ______________________ remember.

Meera You (2) ______________________ think it's in your room?

Sunita I (3) ______________________ know. But I know Nish sometimes takes my bag and he (4) ______________________ ask me. So I (5) ______________________ think it's in my room.

Meera Well, that (6) ______________________ help us now. Go and look in your room, Sunita.

Sunita You (7) ______________________ understand, Mum. Nish sometimes takes my things.

Meera But we (8) ______________________ know that Nish has your bag. And we (9) ______________________ have much time. Go and look in your room, Sunita!

Sunita Ah, here it is, Mum. Nish (10) ______________________ have it!

3 Zane and Noah are different

Noah doesn't do what Zane does. He doesn't have what Zane has. Complete the sentences for Noah. *Noah macht nicht die Dinge, die Zane macht. Er hat auch nicht die Dinge, die Zane hat. Vervollständige die Sätze für Noah.*

Im negativen Satz verwendest du die Grundform des Verbs:
She brushes her teeth. → *He doesn't brush his teeth.*

1 Zane gets up at 7 a.m., but Noah doesn't ______________________ at 7 a.m.

2 Zane walks to school, but Noah ______________________

3 Zane has a sister, Holly, but ______________________

4 Zane takes Holly to school, but ______________________

5 Zane goes swimming, but ______________________

6 Zane watches TV in the evening, but ______________________

▶ Check

4 Likes and dislikes

Look at the pictures. Then write the sentences. *Sieh dir die Bilder an und schreibe Sätze.*

have

1 *Hi, I'm Ollie. I* have a cat. ____

I don't have ____

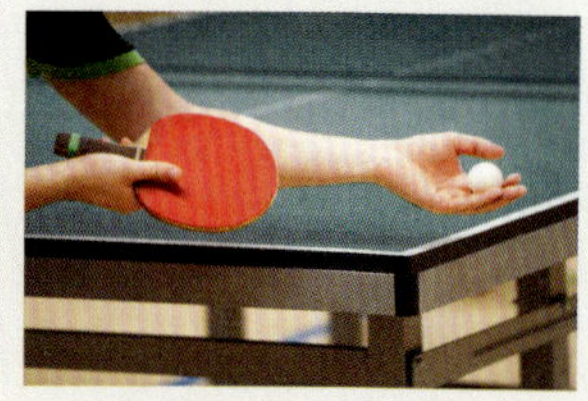

play

2 *My sister* ____

She ____

live

3 *We* ____

We ____

like

4 *My parents* ____

____

do

5 *Mum* ____

____

have

6 *Our neighbour* ____

He ____

► Check

5 Some students in my class

What do the people do? What don't they do? Write the sentences. *Was machen die Leute, was machen sie nicht? Schreibe Sätze.*

1 Radhia and Diya / live / on my estate
2 Kiera / go / to the youth centre
3 Max / read / books in the library
4 Cindy / cook / for her family
5 Luca / do / skateboarding

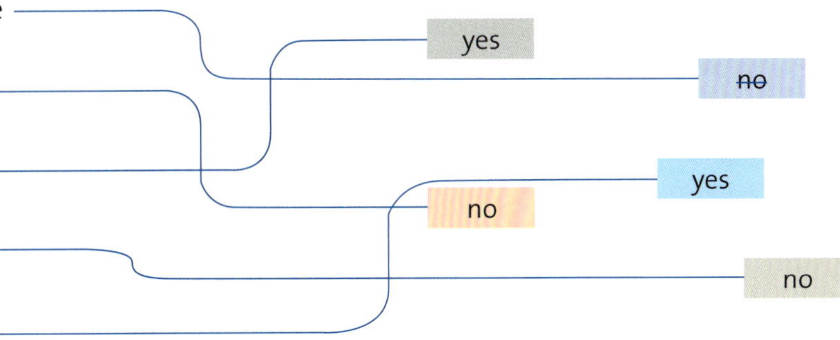

1 Radhia and Diya don't ______
2 Kiera ______
3 ______
4 ______
5 ______

6 Zara's new flat

Zane's friend Zara lives in London now. Complete her message with the correct form of the verbs in brackets. *Zanes Freundin Zara wohnt jetzt in London. Vervollständige ihre Nachricht mit der richtigen Form der Verben in Klammern.*

Hi, Zane. We're in our new flat and it's really good! It ______ (1 not have) a garden, but it ______ (2 have) a nice big balcony. I ______ (3 have) a really nice room and I ______ (4 not share) my room with my brother now! We live near the shops, but I ______ (5 not walk) there. I ______ (6 use) my bike. Mum ______ (7 not put) the car in the garage, so I ______ (8 put) my bike there. One of our neighbours is a bit strange. She ______ (9 watch) me when I ______ (10 come) home, but she ______ (11 not say) 'hello'. Maybe she ______ (12 think) I'm weird!

See you soon! Zara

Erklärfilm

Das simple present: Fragen und Kurzantworten

Fragen, die man mit „ja" oder „nein" beantworten kann, beginnen mit Do oder Does.
Es ist oft unhöflich, auf diese Fragen nur mit *yes* oder *no* zu antworten. Besser ist eine Kurzantwort.

Do	I you we they	+ verb?	Yes, I do. No, you don't. Yes, we do. No, they don't.	Does	he she it my dad	+ verb?	No, he doesn't. Yes, she does. No, it doesn't. Yes, he does.

Do you like bowling? Yes, I do. – Magst du Bowling? – Ja.
Do your parents speak English? – No, they don't. – Sprechen deine Eltern Englisch? – Nein.
Does the library open later? – Yes, it does. – Öffnet die Bibliothek später? – Ja.

► SB p. 123, pp. 208–209

7 Questions for you

Read the questions. Answer with *Yes, I do. / No, I don't. / Yes, it does. / No, it doesn't.*
Lies die Fragen. Antworte mit Yes, I do. / No, I don't. / Yes, it does. / No, it doesn't.

1 Do you live in a village? – ______________________

2 Does your town or village have a station? – ______________________

3 Do you speak German at home? – ______________________

4 Does your house or flat have a garden? – ______________________

8 Can you remember?

a) **First complete the questions about Lily. Then complete the short answers.** *Vervollständige zuerst die Fragen über Lily. Vervollständige dann die Kurzantworten.*

1 Do Lily and her parents live on an estate? – Yes, they ____________.

2 ____________ Lily's estate have some problems? – ____________, it ____________.

3 ____________ Lily live with her sister? – ____________, she ____________.

4 ____________ Lily and her parents have a car? – ____________, they ____________.

5 ____________ Lily's dad sometimes go walking with Lily? – ____________, he ____________.

b) **Now look at exercise 2 on page 118 in your Student's Book and check your answers.** *Schau dir Übung 2 auf Seite 118 in deinem Schulbuch an und überprüfe die Antworten.*

► Check

9 Saturday activities

Where do the people go on Saturdays? First complete the question. Then look at the map of Brighton and write the correct short answer. *Wohin gehen die Leute samstags? Vervollständige zuerst die Frage. Schau dir dann die Karte von Brighton an und schreibe die richtige Kurzantwort.*

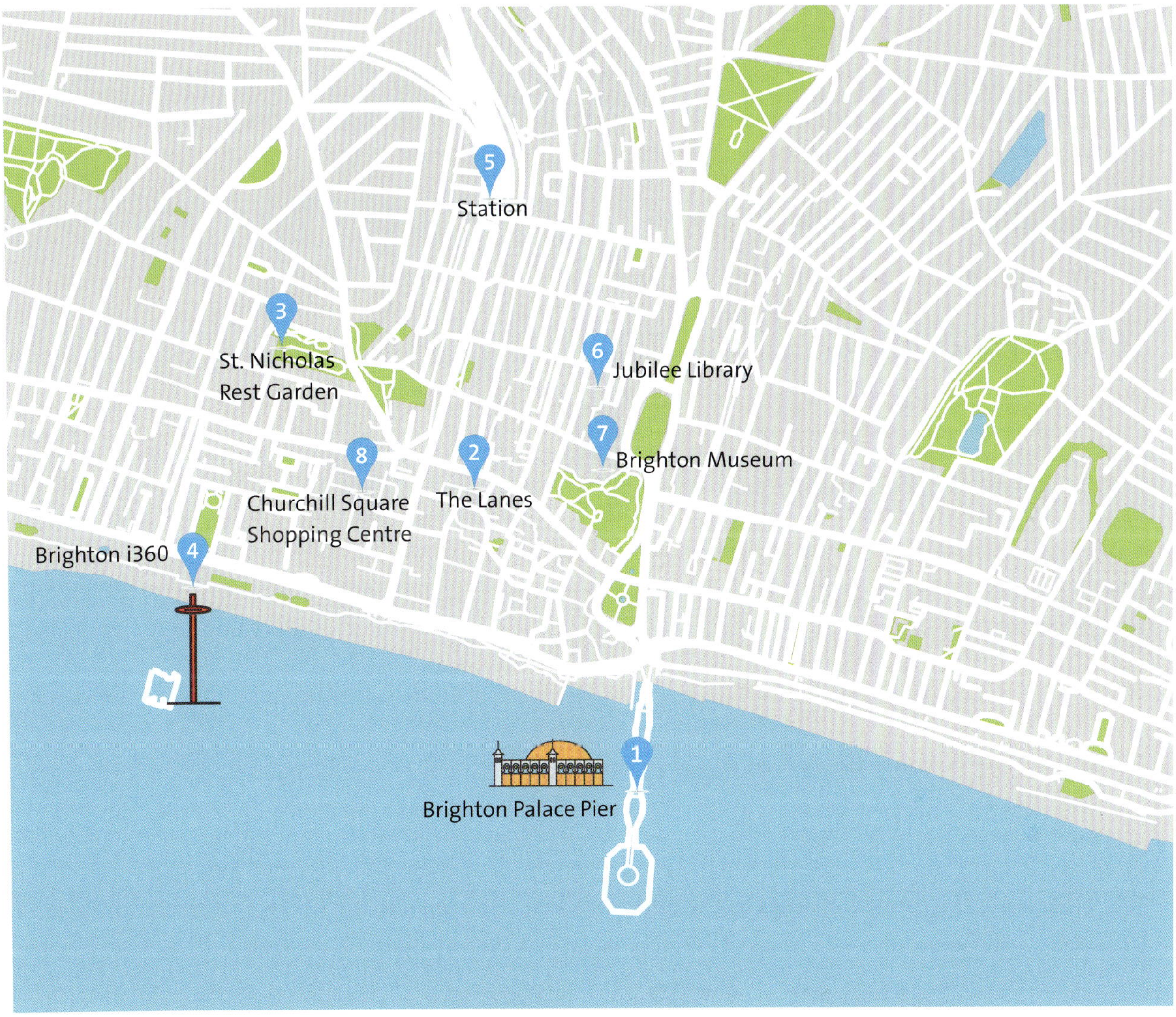

1 ________ Grace go to the pier on Saturdays? – Yes, ____________________

2 ________ Sam and Jo go shopping in the Lanes on Saturdays? – ____________________

3 ________ Mr and Mrs Jones go to Jubilee Library on Saturdays? – No, ____________________

4 ________ Milan go to the Brighton i360 on Saturdays? – ____________________

5 ________ Hannah go to St. Nicholas Rest Garden on Saturdays? – ____________________

6 ________ Phil and his friends go to the station on Saturdays? – ____________________

7 ________ Norah go to the museum on Saturdays? – ____________________

8 ________ Amy and her dad go to the shopping centre on Saturdays? – ____________________

▸ Check

Erklär-film

Das simple present: Fragen mit Fragewörtern

Auch Fragen mit Fragewörtern stellst du mit *do* oder *does*. Das Fragewort steht immer am Anfang.
Where do you live? – Wo wohnst du?
Why does she give us so much homework? – Warum gibt sie uns so viele Hausaufgaben?

Wenn du mit *Who?* oder *What?* nach dem Subjekt des Satzes fragst, bildest du die Frage ohne *do* oder *does*.
Who gets up first in your family? – Wer steht in deiner Familie als Erster auf?
What works best? – Was funktioniert am besten?

► SB p. 126, p. 209

10 Questions about school

a) **Write questions. Put words in the right order.** *Schreibe Fragen. Setze die Wörter in die richtige Reihenfolge.*

1 you / to school / how / go / do / ?

_______________________________ _______________________

2 when / start / first lesson / your / does / ?

_______________________________ _______________________

3 lunch / do / have / where / you / ?

_______________________________ _______________________

4 do / do / in / lunch break / you / what / your / ?

_______________________________ _______________________

b) **Now write the correct answers to the questions in a.** *Schreibe nun die richtigen Antworten zu den Fragen in a.*

In the canteen. | By bus. | At 8.50 a.m. | I talk with my friends.

11 More questions about school

Is the question correct? If yes, put a tick (✓). If it isn't correct, write the question with do or does. *Ist die Frage richtig? Wenn ja, setze ein Häkchen (✓). Ist sie nicht korrekt, schreibe die Frage mit do oder does.*

1 What brings to school?	________________
2 Who sits next to you?	________________
3 What has for lunch?	________________
4 What makes you happy at school?	________________

► Check

12 REVISION Brighton beach

Complete Amber's text with the verbs from the box in the correct form. *Vervollständige Ambers Text mit den Verben aus dem Kasten in der richtigen Form.*

"Everybody" is singular!
Everybody is happy.

be • buy • close • do • go (3x) • have • listen • read • swim • want

Everybody (1) ____________ happy on a summer's day! We (2) ____________ a picnic on the beach. Mum always (3) ____________ in the sea, but Dad doesn't (4) ____________ into the water when it's cold. Then Mum (5) ____________ a book and Dad (6) ____________ a crossword. I (7) ____________ to music. In the afternoon we often (8) ____________ to the pier and Dad (9) ____________ rock. The pier (10) ____________ at 6 p.m., but we often don't (11) ____________ to go home until[1] the sun (12) ____________ down.

13 REVISION At Hove Skatepark

Read Mailin's sentences. Then write Juri's sentences. *Lies Mailins Sätze. Schreibe dann Juris Sätze.*

1 I like skateboarding. I ____________ skateboarding.
2 I can skateboard very well. ____________
3 Skateboarding is fun! ____________
4 My skateboard works well! ____________

[1] **until** *bis*

► Check

14 Revision Weekends

Complete the text. Use the correct forms of the verbs in brackets. *Vervollständige den Text. Verwende die Verben in Klammern in der richtigen Form.*

Zane Where ____________ (1 you / like) to go at the weekend, Lily?

Lily Oh, I ____________ (2 not / know). Mum often ____________ (3 not want) to go out. She ____________ (4 want) to stay at home. But I sometimes ____________ (5 go) out with dad. And what ____________ (6 you / do), Zane?

Zane Me? I often ____________ (7 cook) for my family. They all ____________ (8 like) that. Who ____________ (9 cook) in your family, Lily?

Lily Sometimes mum, sometimes dad. But I ____________ (10 not / cook)!

15 Revision Too many questions about the pier

Complete the tourist's questions about the pier. Tip: Look at Zane's answers first! *Vervollständige die Fragen des Touristen über die Pier. Tipp: Sieh dir zuerst Zanes Antworten an.*

Tourist ____________ it free to go on the pier?

Zane Yes, it is.

Tourist ____________ trampolines?

Zane Yes, there are.

Tourist ____________ they ____________ special activities at Halloween?

Zane Yes, they do. They have special activities at Halloween and also at Christmas.

Tourist ____________ you buy fish and chips on the pier?

Zane Yes, you can.

Tourist And when ____________ the pier ____________?

Zane It closes at 6 p.m.

Tourist Thank you. But it's cloudy and windy. I think it's too cold for the pier today!

▸ Check

Unit 5
Enjoy!

Erklär-film

Das present progressive: Bejahte Aussagesätze

Mit dem *present progressive* sagst du, was jemand jetzt gerade tut. Du beschreibst damit auch, was auf Bildern passiert. Signalwörter für das *present progressive* sind: now (jetzt, gerade), at the moment (im Moment), today (heute).

Das *present progressive* besteht aus zwei Teilen:

be + verb + -ing

Be kennst du bereits aus Unit 1.

I'm / am
you/we/they're / are + verb + ing
he/she/it's / is

Kurzformen nach Pronomen:
- *She's going., They're singing.*

Langformen nach Nomen:
- *Kate is going., My parents are singing.*

She's looking happy in the photo. – Sie sieht glücklich aus auf dem Foto.
I'm visiting my grandma at the moment. – Ich besuche gerade meine Großmutter.

▸ Grammarmaster p. 10, SB p. 152, p. 210

1 Noah's visit to London Zoo

a) **Noah and his grandma are in London Zoo. Circle the right form of the verbs.**
Noah und seine Großmutter sind im Londoner Zoo. Kreise die richtige Form der Verben ein.

1 I **'m / 's** taking lots of photos today.
2 Listen! The parrots **are / is** making a lot of noise!
3 That big tiger **are / is** watching me!
4 All the visitors **is / are** enjoying the sun.

b) **Noah is on the phone to Zane. Complete his sentences with words from the two boxes.**
Noah telefoniert mit Zane. Vervollständige seine Sätze mit den Wörtern aus den beiden Kästen.

1 'm • 's • 're + **2** eating • enjoying • standing • visiting • walking

1 I *'m* ____ London with my grandma this weekend.
2 At the moment we ____ ____ through London Zoo.
3 I can see some elephants. They ____ ____ in some water.
4 A big crocodile is hungry. It ____ ____ some fish.
5 I ____ really ____ my time in London!

▸ Check

Die *ing*-Form: Schreibung

Bei Verben, die auf *-e* enden, fällt das *-e* bei der *ing*-Form weg:

have – He's having a shower right now.

share – I'm sharing a room with my sister at the moment.

Bei einigen Verben wird der letzte Buchstabe verdoppelt:

plan – We're planning a great holiday.

sit – I'm sitting in my room at the moment.

► SB p. 152, p. 210

2 Three activities

What are they doing? Complete the sentences with words from the two boxes. Use the verbs in box 2 in the correct form. *Was machen sie gerade? Vervollständige die Sätze mit den Wörtern aus den beiden Kästen. Verwende die Verben aus Kasten 2 in der richtigen Form.*

1: are • 'm • is • 're • 's

+

2: decorate • eat • look • make • put • smile • write

1

Look! Jody and Mark ________ ________ a trifle! They ________ strawberries on it.

2

Jo ________ happy. She ________ ________ because her mum ________ her birthday cake.

3

I ________ an Indian dish, matter paneer. And my friend Kabir ________ ________ the recipe for me.

3 Double letters

Complete the verbs in the present progressive with *mm*, *nn*, *pp*, or *tt*.
Vervollständige die Verben im present progressive mit mm, nn, pp, *oder* tt.

1 I can see Steve. He's ru [ ][ ] ing to the shops.
2 Debbie is really fast. She's wi [ ][ ] ing her competition!
3 Where's Amina? – She's swi [ ][ ] ing in the sea.
4 Why are you si [ ][ ] ing in the classroom?
5 Oh, why is the car sto [ ][ ] ing here?
6 Great, the weather is ge [ ][ ] ing warmer!

► Check

Das present progressive: Verneinte Aussagesätze und Fragen

A Verneinte Sätze im *present progressive* bildest du, indem du das Verb *be* verneinst.

B Um Fragen im *present progressive* zu bilden, stellst du *be* an den Anfang des Satzes. Das Fragewort kommt noch davor.

Wie du *be* verneinst und Fragen mit *be* bildest, weißt du bereits aus Unit 1.

A		B		
I'm not		What am	I	
you / we / they aren't	+ verb + ing	Are	you / we / they	+ verb + ing
he / she / it isn't		When is	he / she / it	

I'm not going to school today. – Ich gehe heute nicht in die Schule.
Is your school closing early today? – Ist deine Schule heute früh zu Ende?
What is Keira doing there? – She's doing yoga. – Was macht Keira da? Sie macht Yoga.

► Grammarmaster p. 12, p. 17, SB p. 152, p. 210

4 Meera and Ben are away one weekend

a) **What are the problems? Complete the sentences in the present progressive.**
Welche Probleme gibt es? Vervollständige die Sätze im present progressive.

1 

not clean - kitchen

Sunita and Nish aren't ____________

____

2 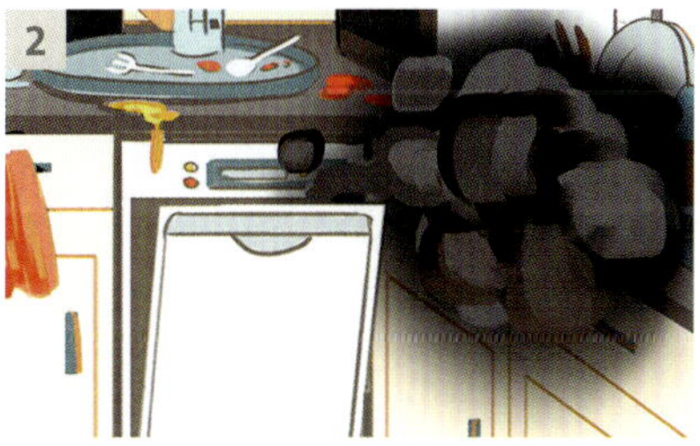

not work

The dishwasher[1] ____________

____

3 

not sleep

"I'm so worried about Sunita and Nish that I ____________"

b) **Meera is texting Sunita and Nish. Write Meera's questions in the present progressive.** *Meera schreibt Sunita und Nish. Schreibe Meeras Fragen im present progressive.*

1 you and Nish – enjoy – the weekend alone

Are ____________ enjoying ____________

2 George and the other animals – eat – their food

____

3 you – tidy – the house

____

4 I – text – too often

____

[1] **dishwasher** *der Geschirrspüler*

► Check

☒ 5 A birthday party

Complete the questions. Then look at the picture and write the answers. *Vervollständige die Fragen. Schau dir dann das Bild an und schreibe die Antworten.*

Um ein Bild zu beschreiben, verwendest du das *present progressive*.

1 ______ the girls ___having___ a birthday party (have)? – Yes, they ______

2 ______ it ______________ (rain)? – ______________

3 ______ the girls ______________ (smile)? – ______________

4 ______ they ______________ birthday hats (wear)? – ______________

5 ______ the girls ______________ (sing)? – ______________

6 ______ one girl ______________ (eat)? – ______________

6 And you?

a) **Are the sentences true for you? Tick (✓) for "yes" or put ✕ for "no".** *Treffen die Aussagen auf dich zu? Mache ein Häkchen für „ja" und ein Kreuz für „nein".*

I'm sitting at a desk or table at home. ☐

Outside the birds[1] are singing and I can hear them. ☐

Some people near me are making a lot of noise. ☐

I'm not enjoying this exercise very much. ☐

b) **Write four more sentences about what you are or aren't doing, how you are or aren't feeling, what people near you are or aren't doing, etc. Use the present progressive.** *Schreibe vier Sätze darüber, was du gerade tust oder nicht tust, fühlst oder nicht fühlst und was die Menschen um dich herum gerade tun oder nicht tun. Verwende das present progressive.*

____

____

▸ Check

[1] **bird** *der Vogel*

Erklär-film

much – many – a lot of

Möchtest du über eine unbestimmte, größere Menge sprechen, verwendest du much, many und a lot of.

In bejahten Aussagesätzen verwendest du meist a lot of.
I read a lot of books. – Ich lese viele Bücher.
Joy usually has a lot of homework. – Joy hat normalerweise viele Hausaufgaben.

In Fragen und verneinten Aussagesätzen verwendest du much oder many.

much

- bedeutet "viel"
- bei nicht zählbaren Nomen, das heißt, du kannst sie nicht zählen und keinen Plural bilden (*music, love*)

Do you have much free time? – Hast du viel Freizeit?

Tim doesn't have much fun at school. – Tim hat nicht viel Spaß in der Schule.

many

Do you know many people here? – Kennst du hier viele Leute?

My parents don't have many friends. – Meine Eltern haben nicht viele Freunde.

- bedeutet "viele"
- bei zählbaren Nomen, das heißt, du kannst sie zählen und den Plural bilden (*one apple – two apples*).

► SB p. 155, p. 211

7 Much or many?

Write the words from the box into the correct list.
Schreibe die Wörter aus dem Kasten in die richtige Liste.

bikes  • ballons  • flour  • fruit  • men  • money 
• people  • love  • oranges  • time 

How much ...?	How many ...?

Nicht zählbare Wörter (unzählbar – *much*) bezeichnen Dinge, die wir als Gesamtes sehen. Wir teilen diese Dinge nicht in ihre (zählbaren) Einzelheiten auf. Dazu gehören z. B. Sammelbegriffe (*food* oder *money* als alles Essen oder alles Geld zusammen), Wörter, die Stoffe bezeichnen (z. B. *flour, water*) und Wörter, die etwas Abstraktes bezeichnen (z. B. *love, music*).

► Check

8 Questions about school

Read the questions about life at Varndean School and Ravi's answers. Circle the correct word.
Lies den Fragebogen über das Leben an der Varndean School und Ravis Antworten. Kreise das richtige Wort ein.

www.mywebsite.example.com

1 How do you go to school?

By bus. But there aren't much / many buses from our estate to town. There are usually much / a lot of people on the bus, so I usually stand.

2 Are school lunches OK?

The food isn't bad, but I think the problem is that we don't get much / many time to eat it. A lot of / Much students need to use the canteen and it isn't very big.

3 Is homework OK?

It's OK. We often don't get much / many homework. That's good because my brothers are at home and there's often a lot of / many noise.

4 Is sport a problem at school?

We do a lot of / much different sports at school and I enjoy it. But we don't do many / much different sorts of athletics[1].

5 Do you feel happy at school?

Usually yes. I have a lot of / much friends. I think it's maybe hard for students who don't have much / many friends.

9 Quiz

Complete the questions with *much* or *many*. Then guess and tick (✓) the right answers. You can check your answers online. *Vorvollständige die Fagen mit* much *oder* many. *Rate und hake die Antworten ab. Du kannst die Lösungen im Internet überprüfen.*

1 How ____________ players are there in a rugby team?

A eleven ☐ B fifteen ☐

2 How ____________ food does an elephant eat in a day?

A 50 to 60 kilos ☐ B 150 to 160 kilos ☐

3 How ____________ rain does London get?

A about the same as Paris ☐ B more than Paris ☐

▸ Check

[1] **athletics** *die Leichtathletik*

4 How ________ colours must a trifle have?

A two: red jelly and yellow custard ☐

B three: red jelly, yellow custard and white cream ☐

5 How ________ people live in Britain?

A over 65 million ☐ B under 55 million ☐

6 How ________ time can a game of cricket take?

A three to five hours ☐ B three to five days ☐

10 Our town

Four teenagers are talking about their town. Complete their sentences with *much*, *many* or *a lot of*.

Vier Teenager sprechen über ihre Stadt. Vervollständige ihre Sätze mit much, many *oder* a lot of.

There's (1) ________ rubbish in the streets. That's not nice, but I think the really big problem is that there aren't (2) ________ activities for young people.

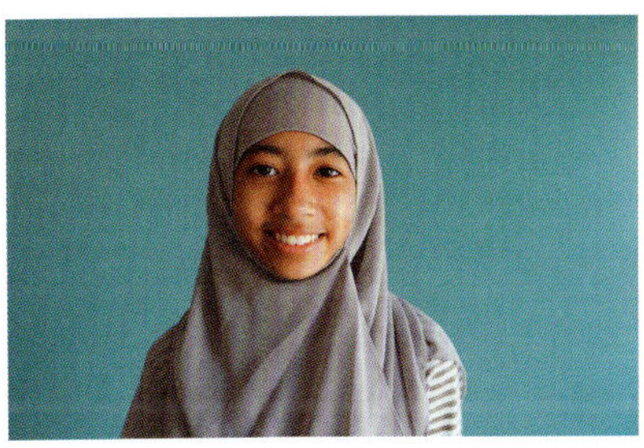

There are (3) ________ cafes, but the problem is that they're all the same. There aren't (4) ________ differences between them. And they don't have (5) ________ really good food.

I love music, but there isn't (6) ________ good live music. And it's the same with the cinema. They don't show (7) ________ really good films.

How can things get better? I don't know because our town doesn't do (8) ________ research on what young people need!

► Check

11 Lily and Zane's picnic

Lily and Zane are preparing a picnic. *Lily und Zane bereiten ein Picknick vor.*

a) **Look at the pictures and write Zane's questions with *How much* and *How many*.** *Sieh dir die Bilder an und schreibe Zanes Fragen mit* How much *und* How many.

b) **Write Lily's answers with *much*, *many* or *a lot of*.** *Schreibe Lilys Antworten mit* much, many *oder* a lot of.

1 

Zane How ______________________________ eggs do we have?

Lily There aren't ______________________________ eggs.

2 

Zane How ______________________________ ham do we have?

Lily There isn't ______________________________

3 

Zane How ______________________________

Lily There's ______________________________

4 

Zane ______________________________

Lily ______________________________

5 

Zane ______________________________

Lily ______________________________

6 

Zane ______________________________

Lily ______________________________

12 What you do

Write six sentences about what you eat and drink and what you don't eat and drink.
Schreibe sechs Sätze darüber, was du isst und trinkst und was du nicht isst und trinkst.

I eat I don't eat	a lot of many much	bananas / bread / cake / Chinese food / chicken / chocolate / eggs / fruit / honey / rice / salad / sweets / tomatoes / vegetables
I drink I don't drink		cocoa / lemonade / milk / tea / water

Example: I don't eat much honey.

____

____

____

____

► Check

13 Challenge REVISION Holiday messages from Wales

Simple present
Etwas passiert oft oder regelmäßig:
My mum works in a school.

Present progressive
Etwas passiert gerade jetzt oder in dieser Zeitspanne:
My mum isn't working this week.

a) **Look at the verbs in blue. Circle the right tense, then complete the sentence in German.** *Sieh dir die Verben in Blau an. Kreise die richtige Zeitform ein und vervollständige die Sätze auf Deutsch.*

1 Hi, it's Chris. I'm phoning from Wales!

Simple present / Present progressive, weil ______________________

2 It's great here and we cycle every day.

Simple present / Present progressive, weil ______________________

3 I'm back from a great cycling tour and I'm enjoying my tea now.

Simple present / Present progressive, weil ______________________

b) **Now read the message in c. Highlight the signal words for the simple present in blue and the signal words for the present progressive in green.** *Lies die Nachricht in c. Markiere die Signalwörter für das simple present in Blau und die Signalwörter für das present progressive in Grün.*

c) **Now complete the message with the verbs in brackets. Use the correct tense.** *Vervollständige nun die Nachricht mit den Verben in Klammern. Verwende die richtige Zeitform.*

Hi from Wales! We usually ______________ (1 visit) places in England in our holidays, but this year we ______________ (2 visit) some friends in Wales. Most days we ______________ (3 go) to the beach and ______________ (4 swim) in the sea. It's quite cold, but OK. But today is different. It ______________ (5 rain) today, so we're at home. I ______________ (6 text) my friends, dad ______________ (7 cook) and mum and Bridget ______________ (8 play) cards. They always ______________ (9 play) cards when they can. Are you at home this week? I hope you ______________ (10 have) a good time. Say hi to your family from me.

▸ Check

Unit 1 My new school

► Grammarmaster p. 4

Der unbestimmte Artikel: *a/an*

Der unbestimmte Artikel (ein, eine) heißt im Englischen a oder an.

Du verwendest
- a, wenn das folgende Wort mit einem Konsonanten (b, c, d, ..., z) beginnt,
  a boy – ein Junge *a car – ein Auto*
- an, wenn das folgende Wort mit einem Vokal (a, e, i, o, u) beginnt.
  an animal – ein Tier *an exercise book – ein Heft*

! Substantive (*boy, car, rabbit*) schreibst du (anders als im Deutschen) klein. ► SB p. 21, p. 203

► Grammarmaster p. 5

A/an vor Vokalen

Vorsicht bei vorgeschobenen Adjektiven, die mit einem Vokal (a, e, i, o, u) beginnen.
I have a dog. It's an old dog. – Ich habe einen Hund. Er ist ein alter Hund.

Bei der Wahl von a oder an ist die Aussprache entscheidend, nicht die Schreibweise, also:

a uniform ['ju:nɪfɔ:m] – eine Uniform ... weil das gesprochene Wort mit einem
a unit ['ju:nɪt] – eine Lerneinheit Konsonanten [j] beginnt

Aber: *an hour ['aʊə(r)] – eine Stunde* ... weil das gesprochene Wort mit [aʊ] beginnt

► SB p. 21, p. 203

► Grammarmaster p. 5

Der bestimmte Artikel: *the*

Du sprichst den bestimmten Artikel the (der, die, das):
- [ðə], vor einem Wort, das mit einem Konsonanten beginnt: *the [ðə] teacher, the [ðə] car*
- [ði], vor einem Wort, das mit einem Vokal beginnt: *the [ði] animal, the [ði] apple*

► SB p. 21, p. 203

► Grammarmaster p. 6

Der Plural der Nomen

An die meisten Nomen wird im Plural -s angehängt.

a dog → two dogs – ein Hund, zwei Hunde

a cat → three cats – eine Katze, drei Katzen

! Sonderformen:

one child → two children – Kind / Kinder
one man → two men – Mann / Männer
one woman → two women – Frau / Frauen

I have a mouse. → I like mice. – Maus / Mäuse
I have a fish. → I like fish. – Fisch / Fische
I have a sheep. → I like sheep. – Schaf / Schafe

Ein paar wenige Nomen haben keine Singularform und werden nur im Plural gebraucht:
people – Menschen *trousers – Hose* *clothes – Kleidung* ► SB p. 22, p. 203

▸ Grammarmaster p. 7

Der Plural der Nomen: Formen

Die Folgenden sind die drei wichtigsten Pluralformen:

1 die meisten Nomen + -s
a lion → two lions
a year → three years

2 -s, -x, -ch oder -sh + -es
a bus → two buses
a beach → two beaches

3 Vokal + y + -s
a boy → two boys

Konsonant + y wird zu -ies
a story → two stories
a pony → two ponies

▸ SB p. 22, p. 203

▸ Grammarmaster pp. 8–9

Die Personalpronomen

Personalpronomen ersetzen Nomen oder Eigennamen. Die Personalpronomen sind:

I (ich)	we (wir)
you (du, Sie)	you (ihr, Sie)
he (er)	they (sie)
she (sie)	
it (es)	

! Das Pronomen I (ich) wird im Englischen immer **groß**geschrieben.
Das Pronomen it steht für Dinge und Tiere und entspricht „er“, „sie“ oder „es“:
I have a guitar. ~~The guitar~~ It's great.
What page is it?

▸ SB p. 24, p. 204

▸ Grammarmaster pp. 10–11

Erklär-film

Das Verb *be*: Bejahte Aussagesätze

Es gibt zwei Formen von be: Kurzformen *(short forms)* und Langformen *(long forms)*. Bei den Kurzformen ersetzt ein Apostroph (') einen weggefallenen Buchstaben.

- bei offiziellen Schreiben
- nach Eigennamen *(Zane, Sunita)*
- nach Nomen *(bike, teachers)*

Langformen	Kurzformen
I am	I'm
you are	you're
he is / she is / it is	he's / she's / it's
we are	we're
you are	you're
they are	they're

- beim Sprechen
- in persönlichen E-Mails oder Chats
- nach Pronomen: *(I, you, he, she, it, we, you, they)*

▸ SB p. 24, p. 205

▸ Grammarmaster pp. 12–13

Erklär-film

Das Verb *be*: Verneinte Aussagesätze

Es gibt wieder zwei Formen, wobei fast immer die Kurzformen benutzt werden.

Langformen	Kurzformen
I am not very big.	I'm not very big.
You are not very big.	You aren't very big.
He is not very big.	He isn't very big.
She is not very big.	She isn't very big.
It is not very big.	It isn't very big.
We are not very big.	We aren't very big.
You are not very big.	You aren't very big.
They are not very big.	They aren't very big.

▸ SB p. 29, p. 205

▸ Grammarmaster p. 14

Der s-Genitiv

Mit dem s-Genitiv drückst du aus, dass etwas zu jemandem gehört.

Singular *(Noah, Mr Lee)*	's	*Noah's dog – Noahs Hund* *Mr Lee's class – Herr Lees Klasse*
Plural mit -s *(boys, Watsons)*	s'	*the boys' phones – die Handys der Jungen* *the Watsons' house – das Haus der Watsons*
Plural ohne -s *(men, women)*	's	*the men's clothes – die Kleidung der Männer* *the women's cars – die Autos der Frauen*

▸ SB Hello! + Unit 1, p. 202

▸ Grammarmaster p. 15

Die *of*-Fügung

Gehören zwei Sachen zusammen, verbindest du sie mit of.
the end of the story – das Ende der Geschichte

Of verwendest du auch bei Mengenbezeichnungen.
a kilo of oranges – ein Kilo Orangen

▸ SB Hello! + Unit 1, p. 202

Unit 2 My family and home

▶ Grammarmaster pp. 17–19

Erklär-film

Das Verb *be*: Fragen und Kurzantworten

In Fragen mit *be* verwendest du die Langformen (*long forms*).
Wie im Deutschen steht *be* am Anfang des Satzes, vor dem Subjekt:

You are English. → *Are you English?* *She is brave.* → *Is she brave?*

Antworte auf eine Frage nicht einfach mit *yes* oder *no*. Das klingt unhöflich. Verwende Kurzantworten.

Fragen	Kurzantworten
Am I right?	Yes, you are. / No, you aren't.
Are you tired?	Yes, I am. / No, I'm not.
	Yes, we are. / No, we aren't.
Is Freya nice?	Yes, she is. / No, she isn't.
Is it late?	Yes, it is. / No, it isn't.
Are Tim and Lisa happy?	Yes, they are. / No, they aren't.

▶ SB p. 53, p. 206

▶ Grammarmaster p. 20

There is ... / There are ...

Mit *there is* (*there's*) und *there are* sagst du, dass etwas vorhanden ist. Im Deutschen heißt es meist: Es gibt ..., Da sind ..., Es stehen ..., Da liegen ...

Du verwendest:

- There's ... mit dem Singular
  There's a cat in our kitchen. – Da ist eine Katze in unserer Küche.
  Is there a toilet here? – Yes, there is. – Gibt es hier eine Toilette? – Ja.

- There are ... mit dem Plural
  There are three bedrooms in our flat. – Es gibt drei Schlafzimmer in unserer Wohnung.
  Are there lots of people here? – Yes, there are. – Gibt es hier viele Menschen? – Ja.

▶ SB p. 56, p. 206

▶ Grammarmaster p. 21

Die Possessivbegleiter

Possessivbegleiter zeigen an, wem etwas gehört.

I	→	*my sister – meine Schwester*	we	→	*our kitchen – unsere Küche*
you	→	*your house – dein Haus*	you	→	*your car – euer Auto*
he	→	*his clothes – seine Kleider*	they	→	*their bedroom – ihr Schlafzimmer*
she	→	*her laptop – ihr Laptop*			
it	→	*its colour – seine/ihre Farbe*			

!

- it's = it is: *It's cold today. – Es ist kalt heute.*
  its = sein, ihr: *our garden with its trees – unser Garten mit seinen Bäumen*

- they're = *they are: They're German. – Sie sind Deutsche.*
  Their = ihr(e): *Here are Dan and Jo with their dad. – Hier sind Dan und Jo mit ihrem Vater.*

▶ SB Units 1–2, p. 204

Unit 3 My day

▶ Grammarmaster pp. 23–25

Das simple present

Erklär-film

Mit dem *simple present* sagst du, was oft, jeden Tag oder nie passiert.

I / you / we / they play
he / she/ it / my sister plays

! *He, she* und *it*, das *-s* muss mit!

Häufige Signalwörter im *simple present* sind: *always* (immer), *often* (oft), *sometimes* (manchmal), *rarely* (selten), *never* (nie).

▶ SB p. 88, p. 207

▶ Grammarmaster p. 26

Das simple present: Sonderformen

Es gibt im *simple present* ein paar Sonderformen bei *he/she/it*:

- An Verben, die auf -ss, -x, -sh, -ch oder -o enden, hängst du (statt -s) -es an:

  brush: He brushes his teeth. *watch: My sister watches TV.*

  go: She goes to school. *do: My dad does parkour.*

- Bei Verben, die auf Konsonant + -y enden, wird -y bei *he/she/it* zu -ies: *tidy: My brother tidies his room.*
- Das Verb have hat bei *he/she/it* die Form has: *Our flat has three bedrooms.*

▶ SB p. 88, p. 207

▶ Grammarmaster pp. 27–28

Die Wortstellung

In Aussagesätzen ist die Wortstellung: subject – verb – object.

Dad	*makes*	*dinner*	when	*he*	*comes*	*home from work*
Papa	*macht*	*das Abendessen,*	wenn	*er*	*von der Arbeit nach Hause*	*kommt.*

Mit Häufigkeitsadverbien (*always, often, sometimes, rarely, never*) kannst du sagen, wie oft etwas geschieht. Anders als im Deutschen stehen sie im Englischen meist direkt vor dem Hauptverb.
We sometimes play a game. – Wir spielen manchmal ein Spiel.

▶ SB p. 91, p. 207

Unit 4 Where I live

▸ Grammarmaster pp. 46–49

Das simple present: Verneinte Aussagesätze

Um Aussagen im *simple present* zu verneinen, verwendest du don't oder doesn't.

I you we they my parents	+ don't + verb	he she it my brother	+ doesn't + verb

I don't like maths. – Ich mag Mathe nicht.
My mum doesn't work in town. – Meine Mutter arbeitet nicht in der Stadt.
We don't play cricket. – Wir spielen nicht Cricket.

▸ SB p. 119, p. 208

▸ Grammarmaster pp. 50–51

Erklär-film

Das simple present: Fragen und Kurzantworten

Fragen, die man mit „ja" oder „nein" beantworten kann, beginnen mit Do oder Does.
Es ist oft unhöflich, auf diese Fragen nur mit *yes* oder *no* zu antworten. Besser ist eine Kurzantwort.

Do	I you we they	+ verb?	Yes, I do. No, you don't. Yes, we do. No, they don't.	Does	he she it my dad	+ verb?	No, he doesn't. Yes, she does. No, it doesn't. Yes, he does.

Do you like bowling? Yes, I do. – Magst du Bowling? – Ja.
Do your parents speak English? – No, they don't. – Sprechen deine Eltern Englisch? – Nein.
Does the library open later? – Yes, it does. – Öffnet die Bibliothek später? – Ja.

▸ SB p. 123, pp. 208–209

▸ Grammarmaster p. 52

Erklär-film

Das simple present: Fragen mit Fragewörtern

Auch Fragen mit Fragewörtern stellst du mit *do* oder *does*. Das Fragewort steht immer am Anfang.
Where do you live? – Wo wohnst du?
Why does she give us so much homework? – Warum gibt sie uns so viele Hausaufgaben?

Wenn du mit *Who?* oder *What?* nach dem Subjekt des Satzes fragst, bildest du die Frage ohne *do* oder *does*.
Who gets up first in your family? – Wer steht in deiner Familie als Erster auf?
What works best? – Was funktioniert am besten?

▸ SB p. 126, p. 209

Unit 5 Enjoy!

▸ Grammarmaster p. 55

Erklärfilm

Das present progressive: Bejahte Aussagesätze

Mit dem *present progressive* sagst du, was jemand jetzt gerade tut. Du beschreibst damit auch, was auf Bildern passiert. Signalwörter für das *present progressive* sind: now (jetzt, gerade), at the moment (im Moment), today (heute).

Das *present progressive* besteht aus zwei Teilen:

be + *verb* + *-ing*

Be kennst du bereits aus Unit 1.

I'm / am
you/we/they're / are + verb + ing
he/she/it's / is

Kurzformen nach Pronomen:
- *She's going., They're singing.*

Langformen nach Nomen:
- *Kate is going., My parents are singing.*

She's looking happy in the photo. – Sie sieht glücklich aus auf dem Foto.
I'm visiting my grandma at the moment. – Ich besuche gerade meine Großmutter.

▸ Grammarmaster p. 10, SB p. 152, p. 210

▸ Grammarmaster p. 56

Die *ing*-Form: Schreibung

Bei Verben, die auf *-e* enden, fällt das *-e* bei der *ing*-Form weg:

have – He's having a shower right now.

share – I'm sharing a room with my sister at the moment.

Bei einigen Verben wird der letzte Buchstabe verdoppelt:

plan – We're planning a great holiday.

sit – I'm sitting in my room at the moment.

▸ SB p. 152, p. 210

▸ Grammarmaster pp. 57–58

Das present progressive: Verneinte Aussagesätze und Fragen

A Verneinte Sätze im *present progressive* bildest du, indem du das Verb *be* verneinst.

B Um Fragen im *present progressive* zu bilden, stellst du *be* an den Anfang des Satzes. Das Fragewort kommt noch davor.

Wie du *be* verneinst und Fragen mit *be* bildest, weißt du bereits aus Unit 1.

A

I'm not
you / we / they aren't + verb + ing
he / she / it isn't

B

What am	I	
Are	you / we / they	+ verb + ing
When is	he / she / it	

I'm not going to school today. – Ich gehe heute nicht in die Schule.
Is your school closing early today? – Ist deine Schule heute früh zu Ende?
What is Keira doing there? – She's doing yoga. – Was macht Keira da? Sie macht Yoga.

▸ Grammarmaster p. 12, p. 17, SB p. 152, p. 210

▸ Grammarmaster pp. 59–62

Erklärfilm

much – many – a lot of

Möchtest du über eine unbestimmte, größere Menge sprechen, verwendest du much, many und a lot of.

In bejahten Aussagesätzen verwendest du meist a lot of.
I read a lot of books. – Ich lese viele Bücher.
Joy usually has a lot of homework. – Joy hat normalerweise viele Hausaufgaben.

In Fragen und verneinten Aussagesätzen verwendest du much oder many.

much		many	
• bedeutet „viel" • bei nicht zählbaren Nomen, das heißt, du kannst sie nicht zählen und keinen Plural bilden (*music, love*)	*Do you have much free time? – Hast du viel Freizeit?* *Tim doesn't have much fun at school. – Tim hat nicht viel Spaß in der Schule.*	*Do you know many people here? – Kennst du hier viele Leute?* *My parents don't have many friends. – Meine Eltern haben nicht viele Freunde.*	• bedeutet „viele" • bei zählbaren Nomen, das heißt, du kannst sie zählen und den Plural bilden (*one apple – two apples*).

▸ SB p. 155, p. 211

Grammatical terms *(Grammatische Fachbegriffe in diesem Heft)*

adjective	das Adjektiv: *good, old, nice, ...*
adverb (of frequency)	das (Häufigkeits-)Adverb: *often, always, sometimes, rarely, never*
article	der Artikel: ***a / the*** *book* ***an / the*** *apple*
form	die Form
long form	die Langform: *I* ***am****, do* ***not****, you* ***are***
negative	die negative Form: ***don't*** *go,* ***can't*** *go,* ***aren't*** *going,* ***doesn't*** *go, ...*
noun	das Nomen/Substantiv: *friend, car*
object	das Objekt: *I like* ***cats****.*
personal pronoun	Personalpronomen: *I, you, he, she, it, we, they*
plural	Plural, Mehrzahlform: *books, child****ren****, potato****es****, stor****ies****, ...*
positive	die positive Form: *do, can, ...*
possessive determiner	Possessivbegleiter: *my, your, his, her, its, our, their*
present progressive	die Verlaufsform der Gegenwart: ***I'm speaking***
short answer	die Kurzantwort: *Yes, I do. / No, I'm not. / Yes, she does. / ...*
short form	die Kurzform: ***I'm****, don****'t***
simple present	die einfache Gegenwart: *I* ***speak*** *English, he* ***likes*** *it*
statement	Aussage(satz)
subject	das Subjekt: ***They*** *eat dinner.*
verb	das Verb: *(to) go, (to) do, (to) have, (to) think, (to) love, ...*
wh-question	die Frage mit Fragewort: *What's this? Who are you?*

Titelbild
Cornelsen/Personen: Anja Poehlmann, Brighton Pier: mauritius images/Steve Vidler

Illustrationen
Cornelsen/Evelt Yanait, Advocate Art: (S. 4 1–8; S. 6 un.mi.; S. 12 1–6; S. 14 A–F; S. 15 1–6; S. 18 1–6; S. 19 1–6; S. 20 un.mi.; S. 24 1–9; S. 53 mi.; S. 56–58; S. 62 1–6); **Cornelsen/Irina Zinner** (S. 29)

Abbildungen
S. 3 Cornelsen/Anja Poehlmann; **S. 6** ob.mi.: Shutterstock.com/Studio Ayutaka; **S. 7** m.re.: Shutterstock.com/Zurijeta; ; **S. 8–9** Cornelsen/Anja Poehlmann; **S. 11** ob.re.: Cornelsen/Oliver Meibert, m.li.: Shutterstock.com/Denis Kuvaev, un.li.: Shutterstock.com/dotshock; **S. 13** mi.: stock.adobe.com/Daniel; **S. 15** un.re.: Imago Stock & People GmbH/OceanPhoto; **S. 16** un.re.: stock.adobe.com/Monkey Business**;** **S. 21–23:** Cornelsen/Anja Poehlmann; **S. 25 ob.re.:** stock.adobe.com/Johnstocker; **S. 26 un.re.:** Shutterstock.com/Hasan Shaheed; **S. 27 mi.li.:** Shutterstock.com/valeryvoronessa, **un.re.:** Shutterstock.com/Juice Flair; **S. 28 un.mi.:** Shutterstock.com/VH-studio; **S. 45 li.:** Shutterstock.com/Upl; **S. 46 mi.re.:** Shutterstock.com/AVM Images; **S. 48** cat: Shutterstock.com/Iva Vagnerova, dog: Shutterstock.com/Javier Brosch, football: Shutterstock.com/Fotokostic, table tennis: Shutterstock.com/dwphotos, flat: Shutterstock.com/Grand Warszawski, house: Shutterstock.com/Ewelina W, fish and chips: Shutterstock.com/Anna Mente, soup: Shutterstock.com/Martin Rettenberger, yoga: stock.adobe.com/Copyright: all rights reserved, michaeljung@163.com/michaeljung, parkour: Shutterstock.com/areporter, bike: Shutterstock.com/YL Stock, car: stock.adobe.com/Ivan Kurmyshov; **S. 50** un.re.: Cornelsen/Anja Poehlmann; **S. 51** (Collage): Alle Shutterstock.com: Karte: Ink Drop, Kartenmarkierungen: oculo, Brighton Sehenswürdigkeiten (Palace Pier und tower): iconim; **S. 54** mi.re.: stock.adobe.com/ingusk; **S. 55** mi.re.: stock.adobe.com/www.figurniy.com/Sergii Figurnyi; **S. 59** bikes+fruit+men+flour+ballons+time: Shutterstock.com/Pogorelova Olga, money+people+love+oranges: Shutterstock.com/Jemastock; **S. 60** rugby+rain: Shutterstock.com/Peterdraw, elephant: Shutterstock.com/Kastoluza; **S. 61** trifle: Shutterstock.com/Peterdraw, people: Shutterstock.com/Kastoluza, cricket: Shutterstock.com/aresdimahdiss, mi.li. (1): Shutterstock.com/sirikorn thamniyom, mi.li. (2): Shutterstock.com/Backgroundy, un.li. (1): Shutterstock.com/Viktoriia Hnatiuk, un.li. (2): Shutterstock.com/SeventyFour: **S. 63** mi.: stock.adobe.com/Doug Armand; **S. 65** ob.li.: Shutterstock.com/Studio Ayutaka